I0607439

Rediscovering America

THIRTY-FIVE YEARS OF THE NATIONAL ENDOWMENT *for the* HUMANITIES

Rediscovering America:
Thirty-five Years of the National Endowment for the Humanities
ISBN: 0-942310-02-0

National Endowment for the Humanities
1100 Pennsylvania Avenue, N.W.
Washington, D.C. 20506
www.neh.gov

Marking an Anniversary: A Report to Congress

AS THE NATIONAL ENDOWMENT FOR THE HUMANITIES MARKS ITS THIRTY-FIFTH ANNIVERSARY, we take a moment to reflect on both our history and our future. For more than three and one-half decades, NEH has touched the lives of all Americans through our support for scholars, filmmakers, teachers, librarians, and museum curators. A long list of books, exhibitions, and films funded by NEH has provided Americans with significant new opportunities for lifelong learning. These resources deepen our understanding of the nation and of the people who journeyed here from throughout the world, forging their diverse histories into a distinctive American culture. As we read *Huckleberry Finn,* listen to a blues performance by B.B. King, or reflect on Albert Einstein's theory of relativity, we open doors to the humanities that help us understand what it means to be an American in the twenty-first century. We are proud of how NEH enriches the daily life of every citizen and pledge that we will continue to serve the nation through the humanities.

On page after page of this book, we see how the humanities offer a panoramic view of the American experience. This book and the memorable humanities projects it showcases are our gift to the nation. These impressive projects help us rediscover America as we encounter the people and the cultures that shaped our nation's history. It is a rich, complex portrait that touches the heart and connects each of us and our families to the larger American story.

NEH is appreciative of its partnership with Congress, the White House, and the American people, all of whom understand and believe in the enduring power of the humanities. We will continue to strengthen both public and private support for the humanities, and we pledge to enrich the life of every American in the coming years through these programs. We will etch our story as a nation and as a people in the memory of every American as we shape a legacy of which we can all be proud.

Sincerely yours,

William R. Ferris, Chairman
National Endowment for the Humanities

Report to Congress pursuant to P.L. 101–152

Contents

Foreword

The humanities are about people. Where they come from. Who they are and how they got that way. Where they are going. The humanities are central to our understanding of ourselves and all other human beings. They are all-encompassing. From them we learn about people at war, its causes and consequences; about people creating political forms of every type, culminating with democracy and its openness to the inclusion of women as well as men, Africans and Asians and all others; about the migrations of people across the earth, their language and culture; how people create literature and what their outpourings meant to them and mean to us; about people making music, from classical to rap and everything in between; about people as artists, whether in paintings or sculpture or photography or buildings, and how they made what they made and why we learn from and delight in their output; about scientists and technologists and what they invented and developed and its impact on the human condition; about the origins and development of business and its role.

The humanities are the history of mankind. As a lifetime teacher of history, I've had countless students tell me, "Doc, I hate history." "That can't be," I reply. "What you mean is you hate the way history was taught in your high school, all those dates and places to memorize. But you can't hate history, which is about people. And what can be more fascinating to people than other people? History is about who they were, what challenges they faced, how they coped and created."

Only through history can we learn where we are. Like a navigator, we can't know that until we know how we got there. With that knowledge, we can figure out and change our destination. That is why the National Endowment for the Humanities has been, is, and will be one of our preeminent institutions. Founded in 1965, it has sponsored and supported research and writing in every field of human endeavor, as demonstrated in readable form in this book. Everything human, in the United States and throughout the world, is touched upon. NEH has funded projects that include books, films, museum exhibits, and more. Without NEH and its work, we would all be poorer.

I once spent five years working on an NEH-funded project, *The Papers of Dwight D. Eisenhower.* I was the associate editor. Alfred D. Chandler, Jr., was the editor for the five volumes covering *The War Years.* Louis Galambos continued the work through the many volumes covering Eisenhower's presidency. The Johns Hopkins University Press published the books, thanks to NEH support. NEH is also sponsoring the publication of the papers of George Marshall. Anyone doing a history of any part of American involvement in the most decisive event of the twentieth century uses those books for reference, research, and understanding. Without NEH, they would not be available. Without them, our knowledge of the early Cold War and the politics of the 1950s would be badly deficient.

So too for the many other volumes of presidential papers, beginning with George Washington, brought to life with NEH support. Our understanding of our own past is immeasurably more complete and richer thanks to those volumes and the many others on American politicians of all persuasions.

The range and scope of the work of NEH, in this book as in the multiple projects it makes possible and supports, is the whole of human history, with a special concentration on American history. It used to be, when I was a graduate student, that the study of American history was a study of white men and their accomplishments and failures. Now we have democracy that is far broader. This is because we Americans are the world. We come from all over the globe. We realize that our strength comes from our commitment to universal education and our diversity. NEH recognizes this and, along with many others, is responsible for this marvelous development. Today, history is about all of us—women as well as men, whites, African Americans, Asian Americans, Spanish-speaking Americans and all the rest, along with scientists, businessmen, musicians, artists, and writers.

I recently heard a group of middle-aged businessmen talking about the waste of talent in America caused by the numbers of college students majoring in the liberal arts. Much better for them and us, they said, if the students majored in business. Listening, I grew furious. I said to them, "Imagine what a world this would be if your grandchildren didn't know Shakespeare. If the name Hamlet meant nothing to them. It would be a much poorer and sadder world. I think liberal arts is the best of all possible majors. Let the kids go to graduate school in business, but first make sure they are educated."

It is not necessary to instruct NEH on the importance of Shakespeare, as this book demonstrates. Thanks in part to NEH's work, Shakespeare lives on as "A Bard for the Ages." Our children and grandchildren and their progeny will find one of their greatest delights in life in reading and studying him.

So too will they grow and prosper and create through their studies of science, technology, the arts, the history of China and Egypt and elsewhere, all helped along thanks to NEH. For myself, I can't imagine living in America without NEH. The proper study of mankind is man. The National Endowment for the Humanities makes that study possible.

—*Stephen Ambrose*

Introduction

You might have gazed at the treasures from King Tut's tomb, or purchased the latest Pulitzer-Prize winning biography at your local bookstore, or read your grandmother's wedding announcement in a 1934 newspaper preserved on microfilm, or been one of the thirty-eight million who watched Ken Burns's *The Civil War.* What you might not know is that all of these were made possible by support from the National Endowment for the Humanities. Acting as the country's patron of the humanities, NEH awards grants to support research, education, preservation, and public programs. The end result is new worlds of learning for the American public.

With the coming of the new century, we at the National Endowment for the Humanities have been taking stock of where we have been during our thirty-five-year existence and what that history implies for the future. The Endowment convened working groups to review the funding of projects in four key areas: regional studies, international studies, lifelong learning, and the intersection of humanities, science, and technology. Staff members pored over grant files and annual reports, and talked with scholars and institutional leaders around the country. The findings provide an overview of NEH-funded projects and offer a compelling picture of the Endowment's impact. We have supported 58,000 projects with $3.72 billion in congressional support; those projects have generated $1.63 billion in private giving.

NEH-supported projects help Americans explore the places in which they live. While we often talk about "one nation," the United States actually consists of many regions. These regions—with their accents, history, culture, and folkways—help shape who we are. Since 1966, the Endowment has awarded more than $370 million to support regionally oriented projects, including the creation of academic programs and centers devoted to the interdisciplinary study of the South, the Great Plains, and other regions. Reference books, ranging from *The Handbook of Texas* to the *Dictionary of American Regional English,* illustrate the complexities and joys of American regionalism. As part of NEH's Rediscovering America theme, we recently launched a grant competition that will help underwrite the establishment of ten regional humanities centers across the United States. An ambitious partnership between the Endowment and private contributors, the Regional Humanities Center Initiative will create cultural hubs where scholars, teachers, students, and the public can come together to investigate what defines and transcends a region.

The Endowment has also played an integral part in bringing the culture and history of other nations to Americans. With NEH support, teams of scholars have created monumental reference works, such as *The Cambridge History of China,* the *Encyclopedia of Islam,* and *The Oxford History of the British Empire.* These volumes draw on cutting-edge research and reflect the leading role played by American scholars in humanities scholarship. More than one thousand translations have made key cultural texts available to English-language readers, helping them understand historical, philosophical, and religious developments in other parts of the world. The Endowment has also been an enduring source of support for archaeology projects, many of which have altered our understanding of Old and New World antiquity. Summer seminars and institutes about the history and culture of other nations equip school and college teachers with the knowledge they need to incorporate international perspectives into their courses. Language immersion programs help foreign-language teachers maintain and improve their proficiency. More recently, the Endowment has sponsored the development of CD-ROMs and websites that give teachers and students easy access to materials about foreign cultures and languages.

NEH has been a leader in helping the public understand advances in science and technology. Editions of great texts of scientific thought, including key works by Ptolemy, Aristotle, Galileo, and Newton, let students explore how scientists solved perplexing questions about gravity, astronomy, and medicine. Interested readers can follow the experiments and problem-solving methods of Charles Darwin, Thomas Edison, and Albert Einstein by reading edited volumes of their papers. The Endowment has also supported efforts to make the humanities part of the curricula offered by technical and career-oriented programs at two-year colleges, providing students with important perspectives on their training. At the same time, NEH has aggressively encouraged the use of technology in humanities scholarship, teaching, and cultural programs for the public. Our efforts have led to the creation of databases, CD-ROMs, and websites that make fragile archival resources available to scholars and the public. Many of these are accessible on *EDSITEment* (http://edsitement.neh.gov), our one-stop humanities Web resource. NEH also works with the archival community to ensure these new digital resources remain accessible in the face of rapid changes occurring in technology.

The creation of new knowledge presents exciting possibilities for formal and informal education, and the Endowment has long provided Americans with opportunities for learning. NEH-supported projects have generated some of the most important advances in teacher training, educational technology, and curriculum design. NEH funding helped create the widely imitated Yale-New Haven model for school and university collaborations to improve professional development opportunities for inner-city teachers. With Endowment support, dozens of colleges and universities established a common core of learning in their undergraduate programs. NEH support of public programs also provides Americans opportunities to learn outside and beyond the classroom. Millions of adults who are working or retired, and no longer engaged in formal education, find cultural enrichment in their communities through museum- and library-based activities and public television and radio programming.

The following pages offer a sample of projects funded by the Endowment over its thirty-five-year history. As you turn them, we hope that you learn a little more about us, as well as the nation and the world.

35 Years of NEH-Supported Projects

The Papers of George Washington

Since 1969, editors and scholars at the University of Virginia have organized and published the *Papers of George Washington*, a monumental collection of 135,000 documents. Forty-six of a projected ninety volumes are complete, with the remainder to be done by 2016.

The collection consists of Washington's correspondence, his diary, and papers from his presidency. It also includes letters written to him. The papers touch on nearly all facets of life in the late colonial period and provide insight into the founding of our nation.

The character of the man who became our first president can be seen in the words he chose. "His writing was not introspective but articulate," says Philander Chase, editor-in-chief of the Washington Papers project. "You have to read in depth to get to know him, then you get addicted to him. The more you read, the more interesting he becomes."

Washington clearly expressed how heavily the burden of forming the new nation weighed on him. "It was an agonizing decision for him to become president," says Chase. "He wanted to stay home and tend to the farm, but he was also an ambitious man and understood the new nation needed him and that he had to do it."

Washington summed up these feelings in an address before the Connecticut Legislature in October 1789: "In launching again on the ocean of events I have obeyed a summons, to which I can never be insensible—when my country demands the sacrifice, personal ease will always be a secondary consideration."

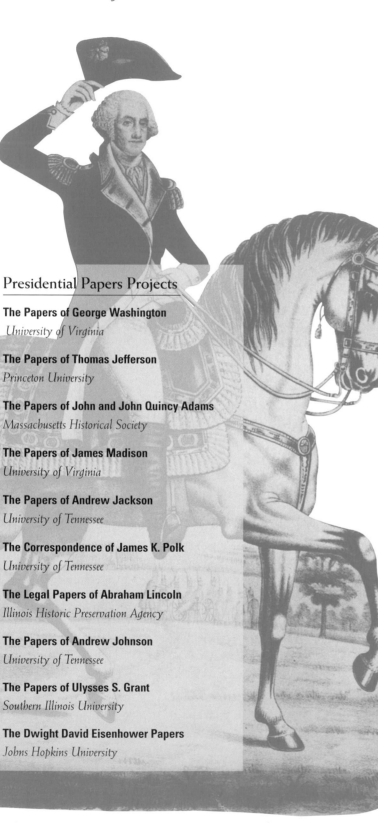

Presidential Papers Projects

The Papers of George Washington
University of Virginia

The Papers of Thomas Jefferson
Princeton University

The Papers of John and John Quincy Adams
Massachusetts Historical Society

The Papers of James Madison
University of Virginia

The Papers of Andrew Jackson
University of Tennessee

The Correspondence of James K. Polk
University of Tennessee

The Legal Papers of Abraham Lincoln
Illinois Historic Preservation Agency

The Papers of Andrew Johnson
University of Tennessee

The Papers of Ulysses S. Grant
Southern Illinois University

The Dwight David Eisenhower Papers
Johns Hopkins University

Restoring the Hermitage

Andrew Jackson's home, the Hermitage, was restored with NEH support. Archaeologists have also unearthed portions of nine former slave dwellings.

The project recently ventured into cyberspace with the launch of the *Papers of George Washington* website (www.virginia.edu/gwpapers/index.html). The website features letters and speeches by Washington, along with synopses and indexes for each of the volumes published to date. Users can also examine maps of Mount Vernon, browse online exhibitions, and read answers to commonly asked questions about the Washington family. Those needing to catch up on correspondence can send an electronic postcard featuring various representations of the president.

"...when my country demands the sacrifice, personal ease will always be a secondary consideration."

Washington's perseverance and recognition of the importance of public support paved the way for the fledgling republic. "Washington was a key figure who defined and symbolized the new American nation," says Chase. "He was both persistent and realistic about the new nation and became a rallying point around which people could look for guidance and leadership."

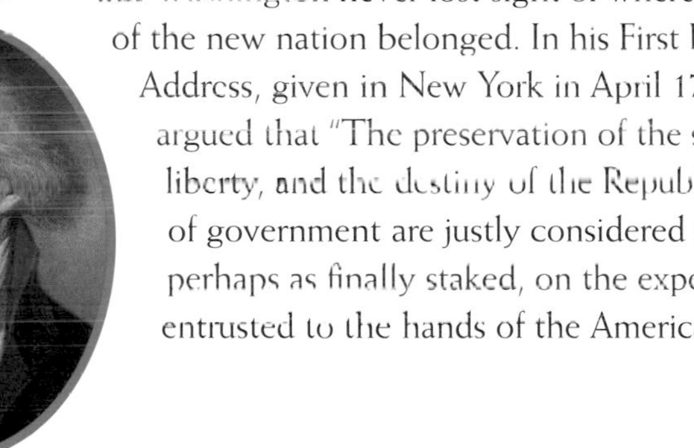

But Washington never lost sight of where the power of the new nation belonged. In his First Inaugural Address, given in New York in April 1789, he argued that "The preservation of the sacred fire of liberty, and the destiny of the Republican model of government are justly considered as deeply, perhaps as finally staked, on the experiment entrusted to the hands of the American people."

Reassembling Jefferson

To celebrate Jefferson's 250th birthday, an exhibition brought artifacts and works of art once belonging to Jefferson back to Monticello for the first time since his death. The exhibition drew 635,000 visitors over a seven-month period.

WE, the People of the United States, in order to form a more perfect union, to establish justice, insure domestic tranquility, provide for the common defence, promote the general welfare, and secure the blessings of liberty to ourselves and our posterity, do ordain and establish this Constitution for the United States of America.

Revisiting the Revolution

Historian Jack Rakove calls it the "American search for a usable past," referring to people who look to the Revolutionary period for solutions to current problems or to bolster a particular political agenda. But something else can—and frequently does—happen along the way. "If they visit the past often enough," he says, "they may start to understand the past in its own terms, and realize that it's interesting on its own merits."

There is a lot to be interested in. Over the past four decades a profound change has occurred in the way scholars look at the American Revolution and the drafting of the Constitution.

Beginning in the 1960s, historians started to look beyond the deeds of great men—Franklin, Jefferson, Paine, Hamilton. They began asking questions about formerly overlooked groups, such as women, slaves, and the working class. The end result was pioneering research that has lent greater texture to the era and demonstrated the profound changes spurred on by the American Revolution. By attacking patriarchy via the monarchy, the Revolution challenged people to examine the relationships between masters and servants, fathers and children, men and women. Historian Gordon Wood sees "a direct line from the questioning of the Revolution to the Seneca Falls convention in 1848," the gathering that launched the woman suffrage movement, as well as to the abolitionist movement.

The shift in scholarship on the Revolution can be seen in *Liberty!*, a 1997 documentary supported by NEH. The film uses the famous engraving of the citizens of New York toppling the statue of King George III. Instead of emphasizing the man represented by the statue, the film highlights the actions of the people at the base. Wood, who served as a consultant, notes that "forty years ago, the story of the Revolution would have only been told in terms of the leaders." The people doing the toppling would not have gotten a second glance.

New questions about the Revolutionary period also revealed the radical and creative nature of the thinking behind the founding of the American Republic. Over the course of their struggles with the British, the colonists gave new definitions to old concepts such as sovereignty, rights, representation, and constitution. The colonists also came to realize that American society—isolated from the metropolis—had become markedly different from the Old World culture it had long sought to emulate.

Bernard Bailyn did much of the work that opened these new avenues of scholarship. In *The Ideological Origins of the American Revolution,* Bailyn showed how the leaders of the American Revolution created a doctrine of federalism by drawing on diverse political traditions, including English conservatism, Enlightenment thinkers, and misinterpretations of Roman civilization. With the Pulitzer Prize-winning *Voyagers to the West,* Bailyn turned his attention to the origins, the motives, and experiences of the men and women who immigrated to British North America. For his contributions, Bailyn was named the 1998 Jefferson Lecture in the Humanities, the highest honor conferred by the federal government for intellectual achievement in the humanities.

Bailyn's students have left their mark as well. Rakove, who has described his encounters with Bailyn as a "transforming intellectual experience," received the 1997 Pulitzer Prize for *Original Meanings,* a look at the historical and theoretical complexities behind the Constitution. Wood received the Bancroft Prize for *The Creation of the American Republic, 1776–1787,* which charts the creation of "a distinctly American system of politics." Both books were written with NEH support.

The Papers of Benjamin Franklin

A team of scholars at Yale University is editing the papers of Benjamin Franklin , the noted American statesman, scientist, inventor, and writer. Thirty-five volumes have already been published.

The Adams Chronicles

***The Adams Chronicles,* broadcast to coincide with the Bicentennial in 1976, was one of the first blockbuster history film documentaries on public television.**

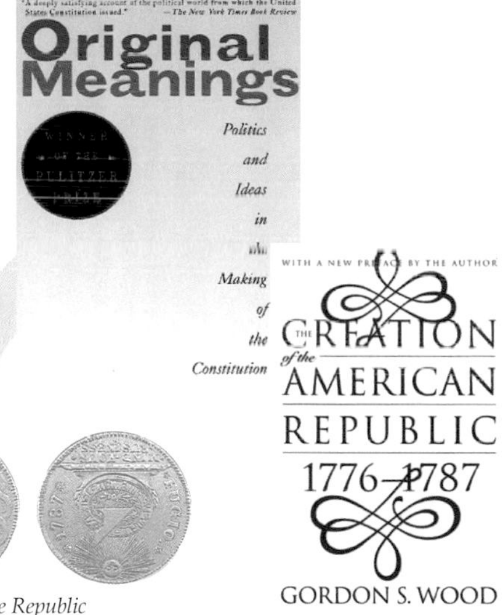

First coin of the Republic

Ratifying the Constitution

Scholars at the University of Wisconsin are preparing a documentary history of the ratification of the Constitution and the Bill of Rights.

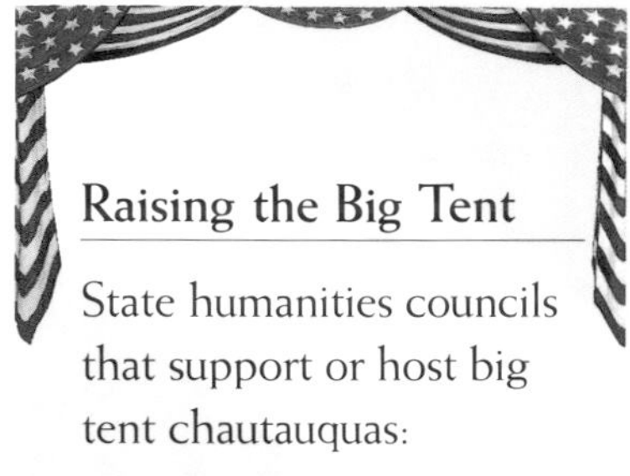

Raising the Big Tent

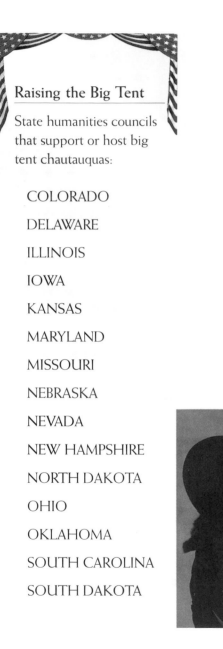

State humanities councils that support or host big tent chautauquas:

COLORADO
DELAWARE
ILLINOIS
IOWA
KANSAS
MARYLAND
MISSOURI
NEBRASKA
NEVADA
NEW HAMPSHIRE
NORTH DAKOTA
OHIO
OKLAHOMA
SOUTH CAROLINA
SOUTH DAKOTA

Big Tent in a Small Town

President Theodore Roosevelt once called chautauqua "the most American thing in America." What began with a group of Sunday school teachers on a Bible outing became a major summer entertainment in Roosevelt's time. A typical chautauqua combines entertainment and education in the form of costumed actors playing historic figures. In its heyday, it drew thirty-two million people a year to twelve thousand towns for lectures, concerts, and moral betterment.

With the coming of radio and movies in the 1930s, chautauqua died out. It is enjoying a revival these days through the efforts of state humanities councils. They pitch their characteristic blue-and-white tents in towns across America, bringing costumed scholars who play historic figures for the entertainment and education of a new generation. University of Nevada professor Anne Bail Howard, who has portrayed writers Louisa May Alcott and Dorothy Parker, calls the experience "unscripted history." After performers give their monologues, they stay in character for question-and-answer sessions. "Questions, or at least our answers, must stay true to the time."

Everett Albers of North Dakota, who was instrumental in reviving the current version of chautauqua, is pleased by the resurgence. "People load up in RVs and follow chautauqua groups around. These are groupies who plan their whole summers around one chautauqua group or another."

Portrayals of Dorothy Parker, Theodore Roosevelt, Thomas Jefferson, Zora Neale Hurston, and Booker T. Washington are perennial chautauqua favorites.

The Clemente Course in the Humanities

The poor in America get job skills—that's all," writer Earl Shorris says with an edge. "But the poor deserve an education in the humanities every bit as much as the rich and are as capable of enjoying it. They just don't get the chance." To even the imbalance, Shorris started a program called the Clemente Course in the Humanities, where the poor learn how to function in society in the company of Socrates, Plato, and Shakespeare.

The course began in 1995 in New York City as an experiment in teaching a college-level humanities course to poor and uneducated adults. Shorris's inspiration for it came while researching his book, *New American Blues: A Journey Through Poverty to Democracy.* On a visit to a women's prison, Shorris met an inmate named Viniece Walker, who told him that what poor people needed was a "moral alternative to the street." Shorris reflected on what she was saying and decided she was right. In the long run, as he saw it, that knowledge could change their lives in more meaningful ways than entry-level job skills.

"The humanities have great appeal to give people a sense of self, to see the world and themselves differently in the Greek sense of reflective thinking, of autonomy," he says. "People who know the humanities become good citizens, become active, not acted upon."

After the first year, Shorris stepped aside as a teacher to complete his book, and Bard College in Annandale-on-Hudson, New York, took on a larger role. The Clemente courses are thriving, and Bard offers credit to those who satisfactorily complete the course. Bard has also made a commitment to expand and professionalize the courses. Eleven courses are currently offered in five states (Alaska, Florida, Massachusetts, New Jersey, and Washington) with a goal of fifty in the coming years.

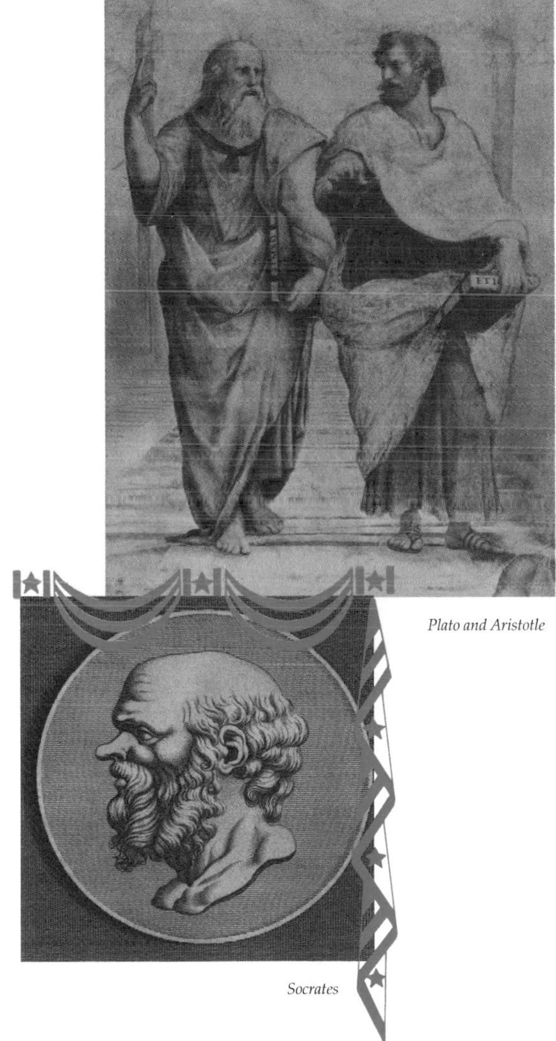

Plato and Aristotle

Socrates

Alaska Shares Its Stories

For hundreds of years, storytelling was a way of passing the long winter nights in remote villages of Alaska. Now those stories are being passed along to future generations at the Alaska Native Heritage Center in Anchorage.

Opened in May 1999, the new center enriches the lives of residents and visitors during the summer months with cultural activities and fills the quiet winter months with learning.

"We are not a museum," says Steve Halloran of the center. "We're not interested in acquiring a collection. The center is supposed to be a hands-on representation of native culture."

The focal point is a twenty-six-thousand-square-foot welcome house that includes exhibition spaces, artists' studios, classrooms, a resource library, and a theater. The center began its first season of public programs in its new facility with support from an NEH challenge grant.

Exhibitions and programs are devoted to the native cultures of the five regions of Alaska: the Athabascan from the wetlands of the south, the Aleut/Alutiiq from the islands of the Aleutian chain, the Inupiaq/St. Lawrence Island Yup'ik from the northern tundra, the Tlingit/Haida/Tsimshian/Eyak from the rain forests in the southeast, and theYup'ik/Cup'ik from the western region.

Preserving Indian Culture

NEH support has helped preserve Native American heritage: The Museum of Anthropology at the University of Kansas and the Buffalo Bill Historical Center in Cody, Wyoming, both installed environmental control systems to protect their collections of Native American artifacts.

The Living Tradition of Yup'ik Masks

The Anchorage Museum Association worked with tribal elders to produce a national traveling exhibition on Yup'ik masks and dance ceremonies.

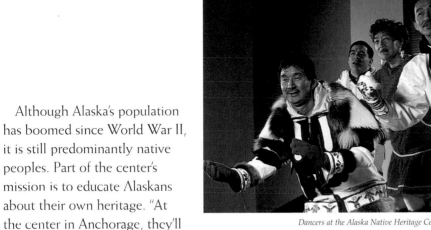

Dancers at the Alaska Native Heritage Center

Although Alaska's population has boomed since World War II, it is still predominantly native peoples. Part of the center's mission is to educate Alaskans about their own heritage. "At the center in Anchorage, they'll have access to cultures they normally wouldn't get," explains Halleron. "The center brings the culture to them."

Representatives from eleven different tribes worked together to plan the center. Tribal elders, artists, musicians, and dancers are on the scene each day to tell of their traditions.

In the summer, activities take place outdoors at five village sites around a lake and walking trail. In the winter, the center offers classes on native traditions and languages. It is also exploring distance learning opportunities for people who live hundreds of miles from Anchorage. Eventually, Halloran envisions tribal elders teaching from their own villages through video or digital classrooms.

"Essentially, Anchorage is the largest native village in the state," says Halloran. "We're trying to take something as diverse as Washington, D.C., or Southern California, and give a comprehensive look at all the histories, all the cultures, all the stories."

The Last Stand at Little Big Horn

The film, *The Last Stand at Little Big Horn,* examines the June 25, 1876, battle from both Native American and white perspectives and explores how the U.S. Army's defeat was transformed by the nation's press into the enduring myth of Custer's Last Stand.

Columbia River Plateau Indians

The High Desert Museum in Bend, Oregon, used an NEH challenge grant to raise funds for the construction of a new wing to house its Columbia River Plateau Indian artifacts. The museum also mounted "By Hand Through Memory," a new permanent exhibition on the American Indian cultures of the Plateau region.

Exodus to the New World

Who are we? The humorist Mark Twain once said that the only characteristic Americans have in common is a fondness for ice water.

From the outset, America was characterized by ethnic and national and religious variety. To a continent already peopled by Indians came Puritans, indentured English servants, ostracized Quakers, blacks in servitude from Africa, Scotch-Irish Protestants, German Mennonites, Sephardic Jews from Brazil, planters from Barbados, Huguenot dissidents from France.

By the 1800s, the inpouring was a flood—thirty-five million people between 1815 and 1860, ten million between 1860 and 1890, another twenty million between 1890 and 1930.

One of the first was the Irish, driven across the seas by Protestant persecution and then a blight in the potato fields. "We can only say the scourge of God fell down on Ireland, in taking away the potatoes," Mary Rush wrote her parents in Canada. "For God's sake, take us out of poverty, and don't let us die with the hunger." Between 1845 and 1855, a million died in Ireland; two million emigrated. The Irish language had no word for "emigrate." Instead they called it "deorai," which means exile.

Lower East Side Tenement Museum

The Lower East Side Tenement Museum in New York City, with help from an NEH challenge grant, renovated a nineteenth-century tenement into a center that offers programs on immigrant life and culture. The building at 97 Orchard Street was home to 7,000 people from twenty nations between 1863 and 1935.

The Shapiro Story

The Strawbery Banke Museum in Portsmouth, New Hampshire, put the story of the Shapiro family—five brothers, their wives, children, and in-laws—on CD-ROM. Their quest for a better life brought them from Russia to America at the beginning of the twentieth century.

Excavating Jamestown

A team of archaeologists is excavating the fort and colonial settlement at Jamestown, Virginia, the first permanent English settlement in America.

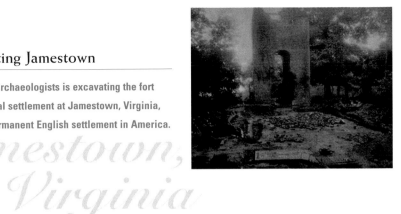

Jamestown, Virginia

What happened to these people down the generations is told in the NEH-supported film, *Out of Ireland,* by the Academy Award-winning filmmakers Paul Wagner, Ellen Casey Wagner, and Dorothy Peterson. Through the stories of eight individuals, the film traces the Irish in this country through the Civil War to the California Gold Rush, and from work on New York's water system to Tammany Hall.

Out of Ireland says that the Irish set the terms of the relationship between American society and the waves of new immigrants still coming in. "America is change," comments Dennis Clark, who wrote *Hibernia America.* "If there's anything that the American people believe in, it is change, development, improvement. So in order to understand the novelty of America, in order to understand the impulse and the momentum that have made America a society of change, we must understand that the people who came here were ready for change . . . Emigration almost prefigures the way that Americans look at society." ❦

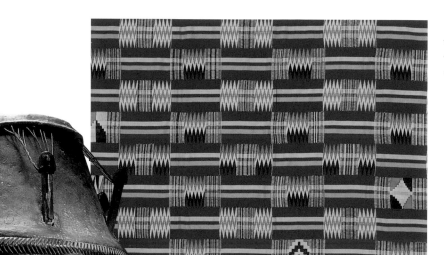

Wrapped in Pride

"Wrapped in Pride: Ghanian Kente and African American Identity," a traveling exhibition produced by UCLA's Fowler Museum, traces how the traditional ceremonial cloth became an American cultural symbol beginning in the 1950s and 1960s.

The Heritage of African Music

The Fowler Museum, the California African American Museum, and the Los Angeles County Museum of Art joined together to host "The Heritage of African Music," a three-part exhibition on African and African American music.

Africans in America

Of all the stories of the men and women who came to America, none is more chilling than those of the thousands of Africans captured in their native lands and forcibly brought here. Fourteen million television viewers heard their stories when PBS first broadcast *Africans in America* in October 1998. The critically acclaimed film follows the lives and struggles of slaves and free Africans living in the United States from colonial times until the Civil War.

"There hasn't been a documentary history on slavery from its origins," said executive producer Orlando Bagwell. "It is the first in-depth look at slavery from the beginning to end."

Over four episodes, the series tells the history of our nation, placing the hideous institution of slavery front and center. The first sale of Africans as slaves occurred in Virginia in 1619, with the institution of slavery continuing until the end of the Civil War in 1865. The film notes the irony of a nation founded on the principles of freedom and liberty, yet simultaneously condoning the enslavement and oppression of a group of people.

"This period of American history is probably the most researched," said Bagwell, who produced the series for Boston's WGBH. "Among scholars and historians, it's very popular. The difference is, among the American public, the slavery period is not well understood, or even discussed."

Subtitled *America's Journey Through Slavery*, the film shows how the presence of the African people and their struggle for freedom transformed America. It examines the impact of African skills on the developing nation, the evolution of American attitudes toward race, the struggle of Africans for freedom and equality, and the influence of African cultural traditions.

The most compelling moments of the series are when African slaves use their own words to describe their situations and feelings. The viewer learns of Olaudah Equiano, who as an eleven-year-old was kidnapped by slave traders, spending ten years as a slave before gaining his freedom in London. Equiano became a well-known abolitionist, and in 1793, well into his forties, he published his autobiography. Another slave, Venture Smith, left a detailed account of his life—both as a slave and as a free man who owned slaves. The story of Harriet Jacobs is also included. After escaping from her slaveholder, Jacobs made it to the safety of her free grandmother's house, where she hid in the attic for nearly seven years.

Many PBS stations rebroadcast the series each February during Black History Month. A companion book, now in paperback, has made an impact in schools and colleges, according to Bagwell. A website (www.pbs.org/wgbh/aia/) has also been developed. It includes images, documents, stories, biographies, and commentaries related to the film. Teacher's guides for using the website and the film as part of U.S. history courses are also available.

"Our hope was to give a sense of the institution and the centrality of the institution to the life of the nation," said Bagwell, "and to explore the contradictory questions of the ideas of freedom in the American democracy."

Restoring Identity

Gwendolyn Midlo Hall assembled and edited more than 100,000 records, including civil documents, manuscripts, and published censuses, to create the *Databases for the Study of Afro-Louisiana History and Genealogy, 1699–1860* CD-ROM . The records, drawn from archives in Louisiana, Texas, Spain, and France, provide a detailed look into the lives of Africans and people of African descent in Louisiana.

Art and Life in Africa

Developed for high school students, the *Art and Life in Africa* CD-ROM shows how African art expresses cultural ideas about abundance, everyday life, government, death, healing, and sacred spaces. One hundred and seven cultures from twenty-seven African nations are represented. The CD-ROM includes essays, maps, music recordings, photographs, and 10,000 images.

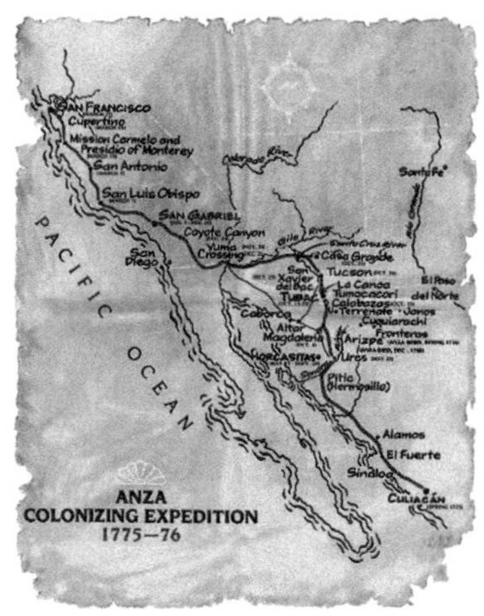

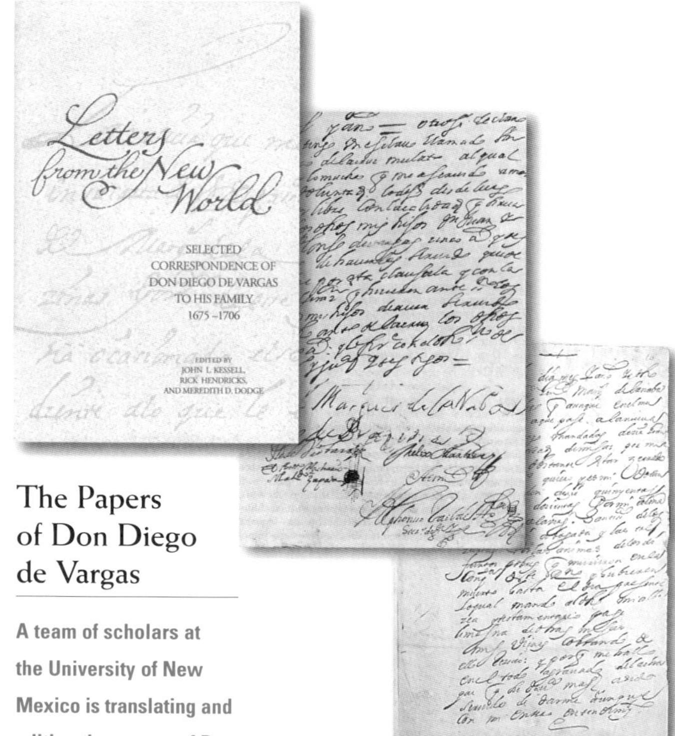

The Papers of Don Diego de Vargas

A team of scholars at the University of New Mexico is translating and editing the papers of Don Diego de Vargas, the first governor of the Spanish colony of New Mexico after the Pueblo-Spanish War of 1680.

Colonizing California

In 1774, a Spanish military officer set off with twenty soldiers, a dozen servants, and a herd of two hundred cattle, intent on finding an overland route from Mexico to Mission San Gabriel in California.

Juan Bautista de Anza

After three dramatic months—punctuated by frequent bouts with starvation, encounters with local Indian tribes, and aimless wandering through the desert—Juan Bautista de Anza accomplished his goal. His discovery of an overland supply route expanded Spanish settlement in California and enabled Spain to maintain a hold on the region until the U.S.-Mexican War.

Anza eventually led some 240 settlers over the supply route to San Francisco. Those who made the journey—a mixture of people of European, Native American, and African heritage—brought with them the traditions and customs of Spanish America, which continue to shape American culture.

With NEH support, the University of Oregon's Center for Advanced Technology in Education is building *Web de Anza* (http://anza.uoregon.edu/), a large-scale instructional website. The website allows students to research Anza's expeditions by downloading diaries, images, and scholarly essays. Studies of Spain's exploration of America frequently leave off with the exploits of the conquistadors. By picking up the historical thread of Anza's expeditions, Spain's role in colonizing California and the southwestern part of the United States can be woven into the larger history of the country.

Indeed, a comparison between events in Spanish America and those in the thirteen colonies yields some striking results. In the port cities of Boston and Philadelphia in the late 1700s, republican-minded colonists maneuvered to throw off the yoke of British colonialism. Meanwhile, along the Pacific coast, Franciscan friars and Spanish soldiers were presiding over a series of austere outposts. There, Spain struggled to establish the type of civic order being questioned by colonists in the East.

What we know about Anza's expeditions comes from the diaries kept by Anza and those who traveled with him, particularly Fathers Font and Gracés. The diaries form the core text of the website. They are supplemented by other contemporary documents, including letters between Anza and the viceroy of New Spain and maps of the expedition made by Font. "We hope that by having the primary documents, people will get caught up in the adventure," says Lynne Anderson-Inman, the project director.

Secondary sources are also available to provide both historical context and avenues for further inquiry. When feasible, documents are available in both Spanish and English. *Web de Anza* offers a wealth of images, including drawings, etchings, paintings, and artifacts from the period. They are supplemented by photographs of geographical sites, floor plans, and three-dimensional models of equipment and buildings.

The website encourages students to be their own historians by deciding what direction to approach the expeditions from: contact with Native Americans, religious zeal, women in New Spain, and so on. "In this sense, the students are using the website to perform the historical inquiry that professional historians do," says Anderson-Inman.

Anza's expeditions had a short but profound impact on future settlement along the Pacific coast. Subsequent expeditions founded two new pueblos, San Jose and Los Angeles. After the Yuma Indian uprising of 1781, Spain abandoned the route. Nineteenth-century adventurers, however, recognized its value: The Gila River section of Anza's trail became part of the Butterfield Overland Mail Route. It was also the last leg of the "southern route" many Americans followed to strike their fortunes in the California Gold Rush.

Mission San Luis de Talimali

Archaeological excavations of San Luis de Talimali, the capital of Spain's West Florida mission chain in the seventeenth century, have provided insight into regional settlement patterns, diet, and religious behavior. Using the archaeological findings, the mission is being restored and interpreted for visitors.

Virtual Mission

San Diego State University, in collaboration with local fourth-grade teachers, is creating a Virtual Mission, which will allow students to explore a mission's history and architecture and, using what they learn, serve as docents on virtual tours.

Picturing the Old West

Denver Public Library is cataloging and digitizing 35,000 historic Old West photographs to make them accessible via electronic database. The library also collaborated with the Colorado Historical Society and the Denver Art Museum on the national exhibition, "The Real West."

Annie Oakley

Sacred Encounters

The Museum of the Rockies in Bozeman, Montana, was the opening venue for "Sacred Encounters: Father DeSmet and the Indians of the Rocky Mountain West," an exhibition on Jesuit missionary Pierre DeSmet. More than 115,000 people saw the exhibition in Bozeman, a town of 30,000.

Film director Stephen Ives and cinematographer Buddy Squires

The Last to Arrive

The making of the West has its powerful myths, recounted in a thousand movies. *Take one:* Brave white men conquer savage Indians and build a glorious continental nation... *Take two:* Greedy despoilers attack gentle Indian martyrs and overrun their magnificent lands.

A third, more complicated version is the one told by filmmakers Ken Burns and Stephen Ives in their 1996 documentary, *The West.* In it, the vast landscape of the West enfolds blacks, whites, Hispanics, Chinese, and three hundred diverse Indian tribes. No one is entirely good or evil. There are terrible costs and enormous triumphs.

It took pioneers five months to travel the Oregon Trail from the Missouri River to the Willamette Valley; it took five years to make this series. Every aspect seemed daunting: the scale of the landscape, the extremes of the climate, epic cultural clashes, human nature at its best and worst, and powerful myths that virtually define what it means to be American.

Burns, executive producer and senior creative consultant on the project, describes it as a collision between "the sense that the West was a place for white Europeans to start over, seek their fortunes, and worship God the way they wanted to, and the sense among native peoples that this land was something sacred, that they were merely tenants holding this land for a larger purpose."

The filmmakers decided they would not make what chief writer Geoffrey Ward calls "the same old cowboys-and-Indians-and-nobody else story." Its breadth is established in the opening moments. People came to the West "from every point of the compass," the narrator tells us. "To the Spanish, who traveled up from Mexico, it was the North. British and French explorers arrived by coming South, the Chinese and the Russians by going East. It was the Americans, the last to arrive, who named it the West. But to the people that were already there, it was home."

Reconciling history and moviemaking proved a formidable task. Written and photographic records are scarce for some, such as the Chinese and Mexican laborers. "We have two masters. One is a kind of historical truth. The other is the need to tell a story and the demands of the dramatic. Sometimes these things are in perfect harmony and sometimes they are not," says Burns.

As with other Burns films, biography became a tool through which to view the force of history. Researchers dug into county historical records to find people who would bring important but neglected aspects of Western history to life. Individual stories—illustrated by paintings, photographs, music, and newspaper articles—were matched with insights from modern poets and historians and contemporary footage of the timeless terrain.

In their quest, film crews were subjected to the same physical hardships endured by the nineteenth-century settlers. One crew filmed in Mandan, North Dakota, with the windchill factor at sixty-eight degrees below zero. Another filmed in Montana when the temperature was 111 degrees. "I've baked, I've fried, I've frozen" in the line of duty, says Burns. "I've been overwhelmed with chigger bites on the bluffs of the Missouri River in Nebraska, soaked to the bone by a thunderstorm in a little tent on the Missouri in Montana."

Use of contemporary footage reflected the filmmakers' decision to bridge the twentieth century. Unlike most histories, which stop in 1890 when the frontier was declared closed, this one continues to 1914. "Most people have focused on the nineteenth century, which is the most colorful period," said Ward. "We made a decision to go from pre-Columbian times all the way to the twentieth century. We wanted to do the whole sweep of it."

Gold Fever

190,000 people saw "Gold Fever" at California's Oakland Museum. A traveling version, funded by the California Council for the Humanities, visited Eureka, Lompoc, St. Helena, Santa Rosa, Tulare, Fresno, and Chico. The 1998 exhibition kicked off California's three-year commemoration of the Gold Rush and the sesquicentennial of statehood.

Basques in the High Desert

The exhibition, "Amerikanuak: Basques in the High Desert," traveled through four states with support from NEH and the state humanities councils of Idaho, Nevada, and Oregon.

Lewis and Clark

Scholars at the University of Nebraska have been editing for publication the diaries kept by Meriwether Lewis, William Clark, and four enlisted men as they explored the Louisiana Territory and the Pacific Northwest. Gonzaga University has hosted five summer seminars for schoolteachers about the Lewis and Clark expedition.

A Woman's War

Richmond's Museum of the Confederacy produced "A Woman's War: Southern Women, Civil War, and the Confederacy Legacy," a traveling exhibition and public programs on how the Civil War changed the social landscape for women in the South.

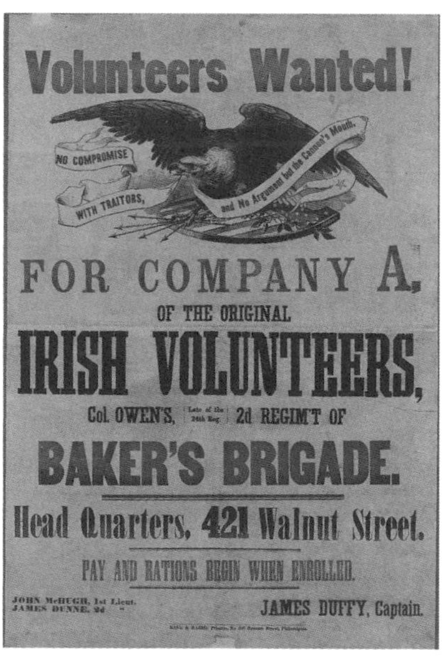

The Civil War

> My dear Sarah,
> The indications are very strong that we shall move in a few days, perhaps tomorrow…I feel impelled to write a few lines that may fall under your eye when I shall be no more…But, O Sarah, if the dead can come back to this earth and flit unseen around those they love, I shall always be near you, in the gladdest days and in the darkest nights…always, always, and if there be a soft breeze upon your cheek, it shall be my breath, as the cool air fans your throbbing temple, it shall be my spirit passing by.

Eight days later, Major Sullivan Ballou died at Manassas in one of the first battles of the Civil War, but the simple poignance of his words would live on. In a moment on television, his last letter to his wife captured the personal tragedy of war.

It was part of a ground-breaking film series by Ken Burns, which drew on diaries, old photographs, regimental archives, and scholars of the period to create an eleven-and-a-half-hour epic of the bloodiest war ever fought on American soil, brother against brother. Thirty-eight million people saw it, a record at the time for public television.

A number of historians contributed to the effort, including Shelby Foote, who appeared onscreen, and James M. McPherson, who wrote the Pulitzer Prize-winning *Battle Cry of Freedom: The Civil War Era.*

Now, the numbers drawn to learn about the Civil War are becoming even larger with the growth of the Internet. A website called the *Valley of the Shadow* (http://valley.vcdh.virginia.edu/) at the University of Virginia gives visitors an insight into daily life in two neighboring counties on opposite sides of the Civil War—how many owned slaves, what the local papers were saying before the war, the everyday rhythms of birth, marriage, work, and death. Like the letter of Major Ballou, it offers an intimate glimpse into lives swept into the tragedy of war.

The U.S.-Mexican War

The war with Mexico a dozen years earlier was the training ground for generals on both sides of the Civil War: Robert E. Lee, Ulysses S. Grant, and Thomas "Stonewall" Jackson. The war also resulted in the United States acquiring more than 500,000 square miles of Mexican territory extending westward from the Rio Grande to the Pacific Ocean. The documentary, *The U.S.-Mexican War*, explores this little-mentioned, but vital, episode in American history.

The Papers of Jefferson Davis

A hero of the U.S.-Mexican War, Jefferson Davis went on to become president of the Confederacy. His papers are being edited at Rice University (www.ruf.rice.edu/~pjdavis/). Ten of the fifteen projected volumes have been published to date.

Will the Circle Be Unbroken?

The Peabody Award-winning *Will the Circle Be Unbroken?*, a thirteen-hour radio series, traces the history of the civil rights movement from 1940 to 1970. The series goes behind the headlines to tell the stories of unknown heroes, both black and white, in five southern communities—Atlanta, Little Rock, Jackson, Montgomery, and Columbia.

Freedmen and Southern Society Project

The Freedmen and Southern Society Project at the University of Maryland is assembling more than 50,000 documents that chart the experiences of African Americans as they made the transition from slavery to freedom. Four of a projected nine volumes are in print, with another coming shortly.

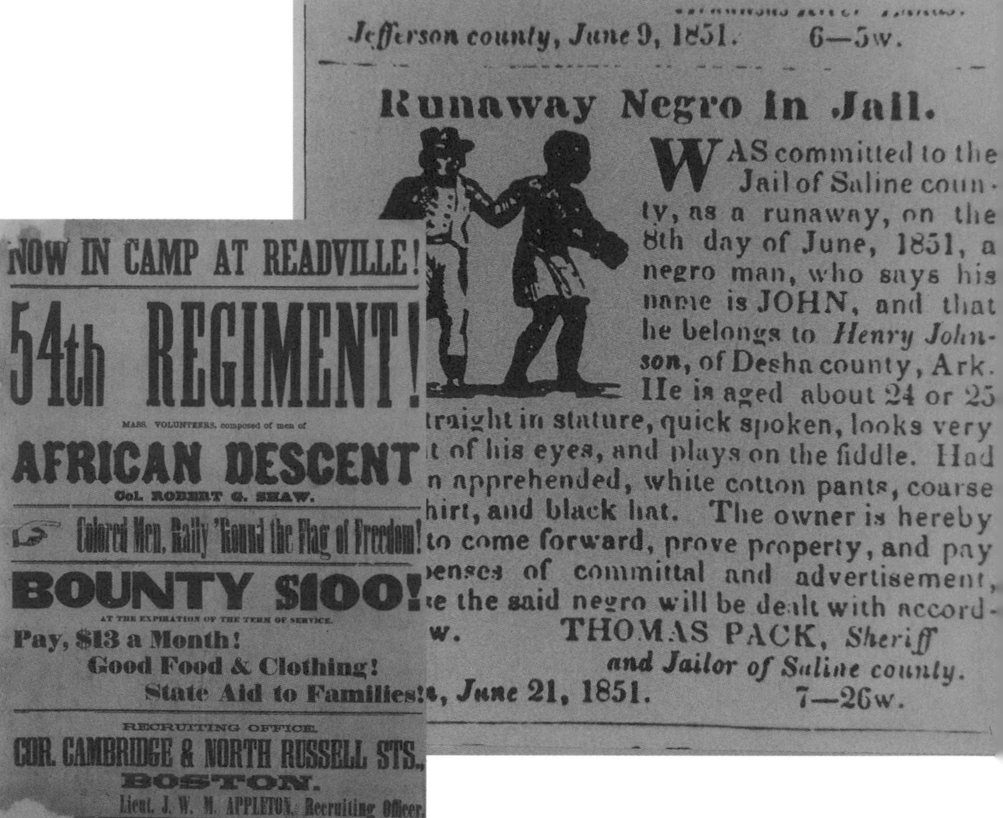

The Battle for Civil Rights

"I will run away. I will not stand it. Get caught, or get clear, I'll try it…I have only one life to lose. I had as well be killed running as die standing." The determination of Frederick Douglass to escape slavery sears the pages of his autobiography. The fire in his soul illuminated everything he spoke or wrote.

Others added their voices to his over the years. George Stephens, a free African American from Philadelphia who fought as a Union soldier in the Civil War, urged others to support the Union. "We have more to gain, if victorious, or more to lose, if defeated, than any other class of men," he said. "Better to die free than to live slaves."

A century after the war, another voice would ring out, this time from a jail cell in Birmingham, Alabama: "We know through painful experience that freedom is never voluntarily given by the oppressor; it must be demanded by the oppressed…We have waited for more than 340 years for our constitutional and God-given rights."

The words were those of Martin Luther King, Jr., written in 1963. As a young minister a decade earlier, he gained national prominence for his support of Rosa Parks and the bus boycott by blacks in nearby Montgomery.

The battle for civil rights in the twentieth century drew armies of foot soldiers—ordinary people who were sometimes called on to show uncommon courage. Nine of them were black high school students who entered Little Rock Central High School in 1957 under court-ordered desegregation. One of the students, Ernest Green, recalls watching Elizabeth Eckford walking the gauntlet to get to school: "It had to be the most frightening thing because she had a crowd of a hundred, two hundred white people threatening to kill her. She had nobody. I mean there was not a black face in sight anywhere."

Craig Rains, a white man in that hostile crowd, said the experience started him thinking. "I think it was that point that I began to change... to someone who felt a real sense of compassion for these students. That maybe they had a right to the things I already had."

When the Lion Wrote History

The film, *Frederick Douglass: When the Lion Wrote History*, examines the life and work of the former slave who became a leading abolitionist, orator, and champion of universal human rights. Douglass's speeches, interviews, and debates are being edited by scholars at Indiana University-Purdue University at Indianapolis as part of the Frederick Douglass Papers Project.

Papers of Martin Luther King, Jr.

Stanford University is editing the papers of Martin Luther King, Jr. Four of the projected fourteen volumes, which include correspondence, sermons, published writings, and unpublished manuscripts, have been completed. At the project's website (www.stanford.edu/group/King/index.htm), visitors can read famous King speeches, including "I Have a Dream" and "Beyond Vietnam."

Documenting Mark Twain

"*I'd got to decide, forever, betwixt two things, and I knowed it. I studied a minute, sort of holding my breath, and then says to myself: 'All right, then, I'll go to hell.'*"

With these words, Huck Finn chooses between helping his friend Jim, a run-away slave, or betraying him for a handsome reward. Huck is certain he will be damned, because he has just rejected everything he has been taught: fourteen-year-old white boys don't help fugitive slaves.

Considered Mark Twain's finest book, *The Adventures of Huckleberry Finn* follows Huck and Jim's raft trip down the Mississippi River of the 1840s. The book sparked controversy upon its publication in 1884. The Concord Public Library decided to ban the book because its language was "rough, course, and inelegant." A critic from the *San Francisco Chronicle* saw the objection for what it was—an attempt to shift the focus to questions of class and literary style, and away from the more controversial issue of race. "The action ... is absurd," wrote the critic. "Running all through the book is the sharpest satire on the ante-bellum estimate of the slave."

Huckleberry Finn was, and remains, the most controversial of Twain's novels, which include *The Adventures of Tom Sawyer* (1876), *Life on the Mississippi* (1883), and *A Connecticut Yankee in King Arthur's Court* (1889). By the time of the publication of *Huckleberry Finn,* Twain had established himself as a well-traveled and knowledgeable man, who disdained pretense and celebrated ordinary people. His persona and his novels of youthful adventure earned him an international audience. While children relished the hair-raising exploits of Huck Finn and Tom Sawyer, adult readers could not help but notice Twain's ironic observations about contemporary society and his disdain for human cruelty. In Twain's hands, humor became a weapon for combating social injustice.

Being a successful novelist was just one facet of Mark Twain's career—he was also a humorist, journalist, and lecturer. Samuel Langhorne Clemens first signed his writing with the name "Mark Twain" in February 1863, while working as a newspaper reporter in Nevada. "Mark Twain" was a Mississippi River term indicating that the water measured two fathoms deep, just barely safe for a steamboat. Clemens had some experience with the river: In 1857, at the age of twenty-one, he became a "cub" steamboat pilot. Four years later, the Civil War ended his career by temporarily halting all river traffic. After a brief stint in the Confederate militia, Clemens headed out west with his brother, who had been appointed secretary of the Nevada Territory. Unsuccessful in timber speculation and gold mining, Clemens signed on with the Virginia City *Territorial Enterprise,* launching his writing career.

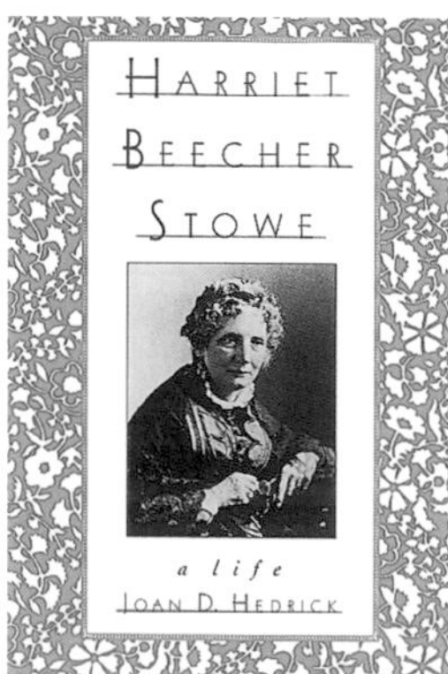

Absolute Abolitionist

Harriet Beecher Stowe's *Uncle Tom's Cabin* (1852) so helped solidify anti-slavery sentiment, that critics cited it as a reason for the Civil War. Joan D. Hedrick explores the origins of Stowe's abolitionist sentiment in her Pulitzer Prize-winning *Harriet Beecher Stowe: A Life.*

O Captain, my Captain!

David S. Reynolds won the Bancroft Prize for *Walt Whitman's America: A Cultural Biography.* Columbia University has hosted six summer seminars for schoolteachers on "The Poetry of Walt Whitman and Emily Dickinson."

Keeping up with the Jameses

The James brothers—philosopher and psychologist William and novelist Henry—dazzled late nineteenth-century America. The American Council of Learned Societies is editing and compiling *The Correspondence of William James* and *The Works of William James.* Being their sister wasn't always easy, as Jean Strouse shows in her Bancroft Prize-winning *Alice James: A Biography.*

The Trouble with Huck

The documentary, *Born to Trouble: "The Adventures of Huckleberry Finn,"* traces the history of and explores the reasons for the ongoing controversy over Mark Twain's novel.

The Mark Twain Papers and Project at UC-Berkeley's Bancroft Library has been collecting and documenting Clemens life. In 1949, the library received the papers Clemens personally selected and made available to his official biographer, Albert Bigelow Paine. Since then, the library has added other original documents to the collection.

In the mid-1960s, the library began to acquire photocopies and transcripts of other items connected with Clemens and his family, bringing together material held by hundreds of institutions around the world. By combining original and photocopied documents, the library created a wonderful archive, including fifty notebooks kept habitually by Clemens from 1855 to 1910; approximately 11,000 letters by Clemens or his immediate family and more than 17,000 letters to them; some six hundred unpublished (and often unfinished) literary manuscripts; working notes, typescripts, and proofs for various titles; first editions and international printings of Clemens' books; and business documents, clippings, scrapbooks, interviews, bills, checks, photographs, and a handful of objects originally owned by Clemens.

With NEH support, the Mark Twain Project is publishing Clemens papers in three ongoing series. *The Mark Twain Papers* consists of scholarly editions of previously unpublished notebooks and journals, letters, and literary manuscripts. *The Works of Mark Twain* are scholarly editions of previously published literary works. *The Mark Twain Library* is meant for use in the classroom and by the general reader. The economically priced editions feature texts, illustrations, and explanatory notes. Twenty-three of a projected seventy volumes are currently available.

Breaking Down Barriers

Of all the reforms on the status of women discussed at the Seneca Falls Convention in 1848, voting rights was the most controversial. It took the persuasive skills of Elizabeth Cady Stanton and Frederick Douglass to convince the delegates to adopt, by a narrow margin, the goal of woman suffrage.

Reform did not come easily. Several generations toiled before the Nineteenth Amendment was finally passed in 1920. The courage of the suffrage movement's pioneers might have failed if they had foreseen how many meetings, rallies, speeches, pamphlets—and eventually, marches, hunger strikes, and picketing—would be necessary to persuade men to give women the vote.

Over the years, suffragists pursued various strategies. After African-American men were enfranchised, suffragists unsuccessfully lobbied for a similar constitutional amendment. There were lawsuits, but all failed. Next they tried state-by-state adoption of the franchise for women, but between 1869 and 1912 only nine western states complied. The movement bogged down until suffragists fastened once again on the idea of a constitutional amendment. The Nineteenth Amendment passed by the skin of its teeth, ratified by Tennessee in a cliffhanger ending. A twenty-four-year-old delegate changed his vote at the very last moment at the urging of his mother, breaking the tie in the state legislature.

Fighting for the right to vote was just one of the ways that women increasingly asserted themselves in the public sphere. Turn-of-the-century America produced women of confidence, unafraid to challenge preconceived ideas about women's roles or to campaign for social issues.

Among the influential supporters of woman suffrage and a leading progressive was Jane Addams, the founder of Hull-House. In 1889, Addams opened a settlement house in Chicago seeking to improve the lives of working-class immigrants. In its heyday, more than a thousand people a week came to Hull-House for English instruction, home economics workshops, lectures, and other programs. In addition to providing valuable services, Hull-House also served as a training ground for young social workers, particularly women. Addams also worked with other reform-minded progressives to lobby for tenement-house

Her Own Roosevelt

Ambrica Productions produced *Eleanor Roosevelt,* a two-hour documentary exploring the dynamic life of the First Lady. The film draws on new research and interviews with her family and friends to craft a picture of Eleanor as a historical figure independent of her family and husband.

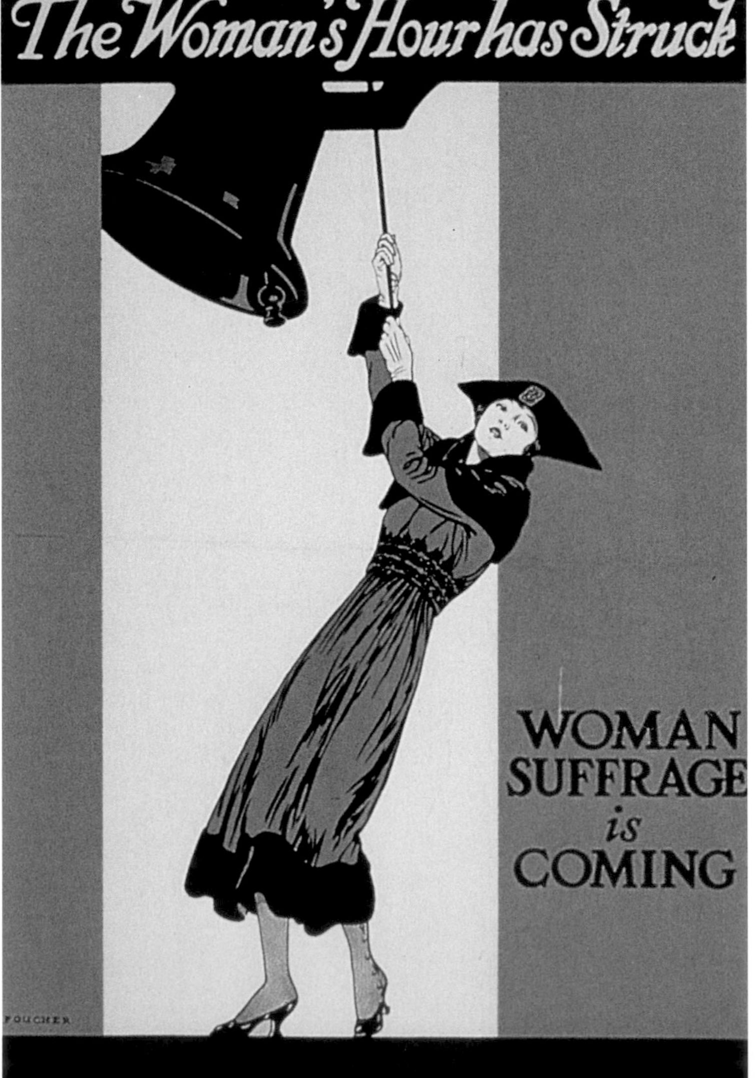

One Woman, One Vote

The film, *One Woman, One Vote,* tells the story of the seventy-year struggle by women to win the right to vote. Culminating with the 1920 passage of the Nineteenth Amendment, the film examines the suffrage movement's leaders, triumphs, defeats, and internal divisions.

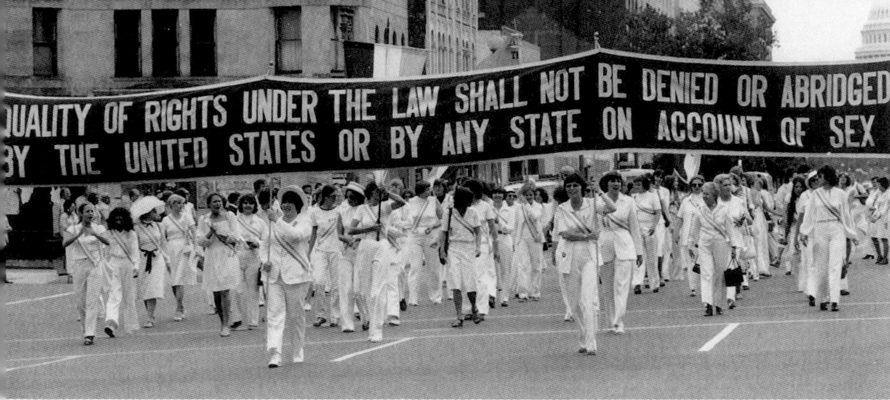

Campaigning for Change

The *Women and Social Movements* website (womhist.binghamton.edu) provides students, teachers, and scholars with primary documents from 1830 to 1930. Topics include how women developed networks to organize reform and male support for women's rights.

regulation, the establishment of juvenile courts, workers' compensation, and an eight-hour working day for women.

Margaret Sanger emerged from the social work tradition to lead a different kind of crusade. While serving as a nurse-midwife in New York City's Lower East Side, she saw desperate women, many of whom were poor and already caring for large families, use dangerous means to terminate pregnancies. Her crusade for birth control turned out to be even more controversial than the vote for women. Carrie Chapman Catt, a leading suffragist, called it "sordid." Sanger countered Catt's judgment with one of her own. "Suffrage was won too easily and too early in this country." Easy would never be a word applied to Sanger's fight. She lived long enough, however, to see the introduction of "the Pill" in 1959 and the Supreme Court's 1965 ruling that "the use of contraception is a constitutional right."

Inspired by the new outlets for women's energy and fresh from English boarding school, Eleanor Roosevelt worked at the University Settlement House on the Lower East Side. The conditions she encountered horrified her, as they did her fiancé Franklin, who would sometimes meet her there when they were courting. Not surprisingly, when Eleanor became First Lady, she championed reforms to improve the daily lives of the poor and down-trodden. Her critics thought she should mind her own affairs. Instead, she served as Franklin's ambassador, going places he could not, reporting her impressions and making suggestions. After Franklin's death, President Truman appointed her as a delegate to the United Nations. Eleanor put her reputation and political savvy to work, playing a key role in the drafting of the 1948 International Declaration on Human Rights.

In the one hundred years since Seneca Falls, women went from demanding voting rights to drafting international declarations prescribing political and civic liberties. ❧

In Pursuit of a Common Goal

***The Papers of Elizabeth Cady Stanton and Susan B. Anthony* are being prepared by scholars at Rutgers University. Stanton and Anthony were two tireless champions of the suffragist movement.**

Family Planning Pioneer

***Margaret Sanger*, a ninety-minute documentary by Cobblestone Films, charts the life of the pioneering birth control advocate, exploring the forces that shaped Sanger and her movement. A four-volume edition of Sanger's papers is being prepared by scholars at New York University (www.nyu.edu/projects/sanger/).**

Assembling Jane Addams

Print and microfilm versions of *The Jane Addams Papers* are being edited by a team of scholars at Duke University. In 1989, the centennial anniversary of Hull-House, the University of Illinois at Chicago hosted a series of programs and an exhibition on Jane Addams and her work. The university also received support to preserve the Jane Addams/Hull-House photographic collection.

Showdown on the Shop Floor

As America entered the Industrial Age, its workplaces spawned ambitious young men, some of them burning to make fortunes of their own, others casting their lot with the men in the plants.

One young entrepreneur was a Scots lad from Dunfermline, whose family became impoverished when steam-powered looms put his father out of work as a weaver. The boy immigrated to the United States; at thirteen he was a stoker in a Pittsburgh textile factory. He became a telegraph messenger, a railroad executive, a steelmaker, and eventually the richest man in the world. Then he gave his millions away. His name was Andrew Carnegie.

Another immigrant, a young cigar maker from London, would take a different path. Samuel Gompers worked the other side of the Industrial Revolution. He pulled together carpenters, miners, machinists, typographers, garment workers, and others into an economic force that fought for collective bargaining, a minimum wage, and the eight-hour working day. He became a towering figure in the American labor movement for half a century and the first president of the American Federation of Labor.

By 1894, union strength was such that Congress made Labor Day a national holiday. In New York City, where there had been local observances for a dozen years, some of the women workers were embarrassed to march. As one explained, "they have very poor clothes, many of them are little better than rags." "So much the better," responded another. "Let them march in their rags so that the New York public may see how they are treated." Indeed the women marched, along with 12,000 other workers, as half the city watched.

But unionism itself was to have a stormy path. It took until the middle of the twentieth century for the American Federation of Labor to merge with its archrival, the Congress of Industrial Unions, and speak with a united voice.

Steely Determination

The life of Andrew Carnegie is told in the two-hour film, *The Richest Man in the World*. Investing in railroads and steel, Carnegie was one of the small number of nineteenth-century industrialists to rise from "rags to riches." Carnegie's 1892 battle with the union at his Homestead steel plant resulted in one of the most violent strikes in American labor history.

Living Her Own Life

An influential feminist and well-known anarchist of her day, Emma Goldman championed union organization and the eight-hour working day. The University of California, Berkeley (http://sunsite.berkeley.edu/Goldman/) prepared a sixty-nine-reel microfilm collection of Goldman's papers, gathered from around the world.

Working the Assembly Line

The Henry Ford Museum and Greenfield Village's permanent exhibition, "Made in America," tells the history of American manufacturing. The exhibition features 1500 artifacts plus nine hands-on activities, five operating machines and engines, and fourteen audio-visual presentations.

Organizing Labor

The University of Maryland is preparing print and microfilm versions of *The Samuel Gompers Papers* (www.inform.umd.edu/HIST/Gompers/web1.html). Seven volumes and two microfilm editions documenting American labor history are currently available.

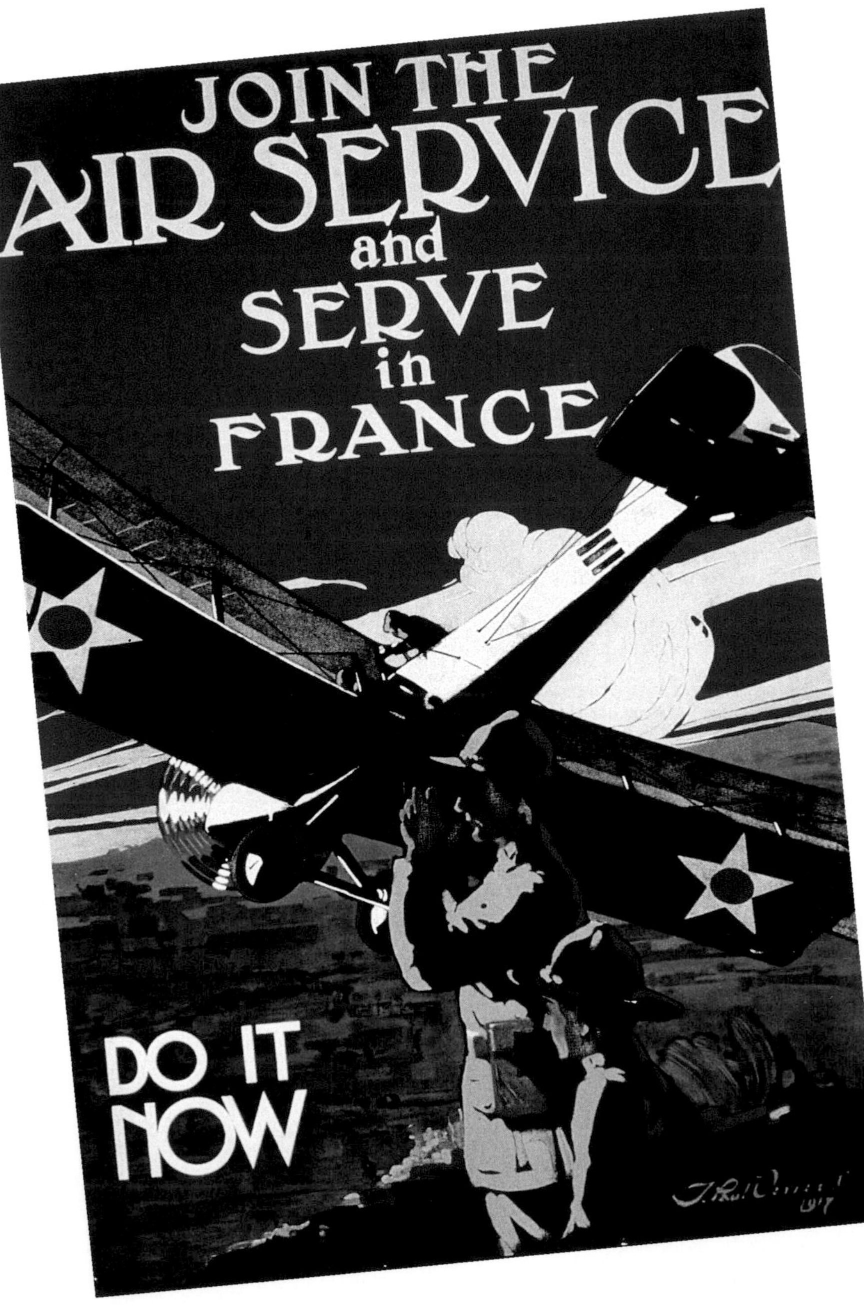

The Knock on the Door

On the eleventh day of the eleventh month of 1918, the guns of the Great War fell silent. In their place the bells of armistice rang out in towns and villages all across Western Europe. On that day, in the English town of Shrewsbury, Tom and Susan Owen received a knock on their door. A message had arrived that they had hoped for two years never to hear, certainly not this near to the end of the war. The telegram brought cruel news that just one week earlier, as the long-awaited peace was being negotiated, their son Wilfred had been killed in action. He had died of machine gun fire on the banks of a muddy canal in France.

Owen was one of England's most promising young poets. When war broke out, his verse reflected a romantic view of battle that was common among the young men of 1914.

O meet it is and passing sweet
To live in peace with others,
But sweeter still and far more meet
To die in war for brothers.

Four years later, Owen's poetry reflected a quite different reality.

So, soon they topped the hill, and raced together
Over an open stretch of herb and heather
Exposed. And instantly the whole sky burned
With fury against them; earth set sudden cups
In thousands for their blood; and the green slope
Chasmed and steepened sheer to infinite space.

Wilfred Owen was among the last of the war's official victims. By then the war had already claimed an unimaginable number of casualties. Two million German dead. Almost two million Russians. Well over one million French. One out of eight of those who served died. Like Wilfred Owen, each of those nine million left behind loved ones: wives, parents, and children whose own lives would be forever shattered.

Vera Brittain was a volunteer nurse in a London hospital. She had already lost her fiancé Roland in late 1915, and harbored hopes that at least her younger brother Edward would be spared. When she read of heavy fighting in June 1918 on the Italian front where her brother was serving, she had a premonition that he was gone too:

Wilfred Owen

I had just announced to my father, as we sat over tea in the dining-room, that I really must do up Edward's papers and take them to the post office before it closed for the weekend, when there came the sudden loud clattering at the front-door knocker that always meant a telegram …

I knew what was in the telegram—I had known for a week—but because the persistent hopefulness of the human heart refuses to allow intuitive certainty to persuade the reason of that which it knows, I opened and read it in a tearing anguish of suspense.

"Regret to inform you Captain E. H. Brittain M.C. killed in action Italy June 15th."

The knock on the door was democratic. The prominent and the rich knew it as did the ordinary citizen.

The Great War was a great tragedy. The dimension of human suffering alone confirms this. But there is more tragedy to this sad story, for the sacrifices did not deliver a resolution. Like Owen's family, the world soon realized that it was not safe with the news that war had ended, for in the war were sown the seeds of an even greater conflict.

—From THE GREAT WAR AND THE SHAPING OF THE TWENTIETH CENTURY

The Great War and the Shaping of the Twentieth Century, *an eight-hour NEH-supported documentary, was coproduced by KCET/Los Angeles and the BBC in association with the Imperial War Museum. The film's website (www.pbs.org/greatwar/) includes interviews with historians about the conflict, an interactive timeline, and evolving maps of Europe.*

The Great War and Modern Memory

This year marks the twenty-fifth anniversary of Paul Fussell's book, *The Great War and Modern Memory*. The book won the National Book Award and the National Book Critics Circle Award; it was recently named by the Modern Library as one of the twentieth century's 100 Best Non-Fiction Books.

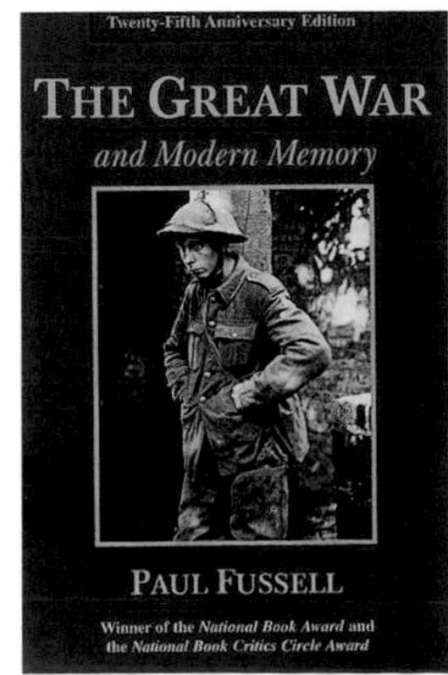

The Remote Sound of War

Edith Wharton would remember July 30, 1914, as a day when she felt singularly attuned, in a sort of ultimate peacefulness, to everything that was enduring, strong, and beautiful in France. Motoring north from Poitiers, the party had lunch by the roadside, under apple trees at the edge of a field. In the noonday quiet Edith surveyed the "sober disciplined landscape" which spoke to her of the steady attachment to the soil of generations of workers in the field. The serenity of the scene, she thought, simply smiled away the war rumors which had hung around them for several days. It was just over a month since the Austrian Archduke Franz Ferdinand, the heir to the Hapsburg throne, had been assassinated at Sarajevo. Austria-Hungary had declared war on Serbia, and on the day Edith and Berry reached Poitiers, Russia had mobilized for the defense of her little neighbor Germany seized the occasion to issue Russia an ultimatum; two days later Germany and Russia were at war.

To the travelers all this seemed unreal, remote stage posturings. The town of Chartres, which they entered at four in the afternoon, was saturated with sunlight, and the cathedral was an extraordinary contrast of dark shadows below, pricked only by a few altar lights, and above "great sheets and showers of colour" from the amazing stained-glass windows. "All that a great cathedral can be, all the meanings it can express, all the tranquilising power it can breathe upon the soul," Edith wrote, " … the cathedral of Chartres gave us in that perfect hour." It was sunset when they drove into Paris. There was a pink-blue luster on the Seine; the Boise held the stillness of a summer evening; the currents of life flowed evenly and quietly along the avenues. At that moment in history, in Edith Wharton's sad imaginative words, "the great city, so made for peace and art and all humanest graces, seemed to lie by her river-side like a princess guarded by the watchful giant of the Eiffel Tower."

—From R.W.B. Lewis's Pulitzer Prize-winning book, *Edith Wharton: A Biography*

Zelda and F. Scott Fitzgerald

Recovering Fitzgerald

Scholars who study F. Scott Fitzgerald have long known about the existence of an underlying version of The Great Gatsby. *But the text of this version, called* Trimalchio *after the ostentatious party-giver in the* Satyricon of Petronius, *had never been formally published or assessed. James L.W. West III, Distinguished Professor of English at Pennsylvania State University, used the galley proofs of* Gatsby *to reconstruct the original manuscript. Below, West talks about how* Trimalchio *differs from* Gatsby.

Reading F. Scott Fitzgerald's *Trimalchio,* an early and complete version of *The Great Gatsby,* is like listening to a well-known musical composition, but played in a different key and with an alternate bridge passage. A theme that one usually hears in the middle movement is now heard in the last. Familiar leitmotifs play through the work but appear at unexpected moments. Several favorite passages are missing, but new combinations and sequences, recognizably from the hand of the composer, are present. To the knowledgeable listener it is like hearing the same work and yet a different work.

Trimalchio is not the same story as *The Great Gatsby*. They are similar: the first two chapters of both books are almost identical; both novels have nine chapters and are narrated by Nick Carraway; both explore the effects of money and social status on human behavior and morality. The green light stands at the end of the Buchanans' dock in both novels; Dan Cody and Meyer Wolfshiem are in both texts; Jay Gatsby gives his fabulous parties and uses the term "old sport" in both narratives. *Trimalchio* and *The Great Gatsby* both include the famous guest list for Gatsby's parties, and there is money in Daisy's voice in both novels.

There are crucial differences, however. Nick Carraway is not the same in *Trimalchio*: he is more snobbish, less likable, and self-deprecating. Nick's love affair with Jordan Baker is traced in greater detail in *Trimalchio,* and we see more clearly why they are drawn to each other. Jordan's personality is more fully revealed: She, like Nick, is not as attractive a character, and the two of them are more clearly complicit in Daisy's affair with Gatsby, and in the wreckage that follows. The reader is more aware in *Trimalchio* of Gatsby's courting of celebrities—and of Tom and Daisy's aversion to them. The confrontation between Tom and Gatsby in the Plaza Hotel is handled differently in *Trimalchio* (Gatsby is less convincingly defeated), and the mechanics of moving the characters from Long Island to central Manhattan is managed in a less roundabout way.

innuendo, and obviously under the impression that sooner or later Jordan was going to yield him up her person to a greater or lesser degree. Instead of rambling this party had preserved a dignified homogeneity, and assumed to itself the function of representing the staid nobility of the country-side—West Egg condescending to East Egg, and carefully on guard against its spectroscopic gayety.

The men—I had known one of them at New Haven—all affected the Oxford mush-mouth accent but, as I presently discovered, they were by no means snobs.

"Entering son Eton and Groton," remarked my friend. "Prob'ly send him Andovah, though. Wouldn't want him to turn out snob."

"Good idea," I suggested. "Why not send him to a high school in New York?"

He laughed.

"I've been out with those two girls you were talking to," announced the undergraduate to Jordan. "God, how they do bore me!"

"Who?" she asked absently.

"Those two girls in yellow. I'd rather pass my afternoons in the glass parlors at Westover."

"That may be true," answered Jordan. "We may be the kind of girls you go around with, but those are the kind of girl you marry."

She put her plate on a chair, and leaning back and smiling a wan smile, regarded the dark, open sky. At this table the conversation was turning upon the movie star. Some one had heard her refer to her legs as "limbs," and so we all laughed because they said legs and not limbs, which put them at a big advantage. The women were more kind about her after they heard that she said limbs.

"Come on," whispered Jordan to me. "Let's get out."

We got up, and she explained that we were going to find the host: I had never met him, she said, and it was making me uneasy. The undergraduate nodded in a cynical, melancholy way.

The bar, where we glanced first, was crowded.

Galley from Trimalchio

The Cambridge Edition of the Works of
F. SCOTT FITZGERALD
Edited by James L. W. West III
TRIMALCHIO
An Early Version of
The Great Gatsby
F. Scott Fitzgerald

Most important, the unfolding of Jay Gatsby's character is timed and executed in a wholly different fashion in *Trimalchio*. He remains shadowy and indistinct for a longer time; he gives Nick a few hints about his background, but not many. His past is a mystery until after Daisy runs down Myrtle Wilson while driving his yellow car. Some hours later, distraught and exhausted, Gatsby reveals his past to Nick in a beautifully rendered early-morning conversation—a sort of confessional scene.

All of this gives scholars, teachers, and students new things to talk about. (Most of us think we know by now approximately what the green light stands for.) Literary critics will debate whether the changes Fitzgerald made improved the story. Students will see the same cast of characters but will observe them through an alternate set of lenses and filters. Readers will have a new party at Gatsby's to study—a masquerade affair in Chapter VI—and will see Fitzgerald's hero, Jay Gatsby, revealed in a more direct way.

Jazzing It up in Paris

The Jazz Age in Paris, 1914–1940, **an exhibition produced by the American Library Association and the Smithsonian Institution, is traveling to twenty-eight libraries across the country on a two-year tour. Musicians, expatriate authors, avant-garde artists, flappers, and socialites disillusioned by the war came together at Parisian jazz clubs.**

A National Pastime

Episode four of Ken Burns's film *Baseball* focuses on the 1920s, the decade in which Babe Ruth became the best-known baseball player in history. Over the course of "nine innings," *Baseball* charts the evolution of the game that has been called America's national pastime.

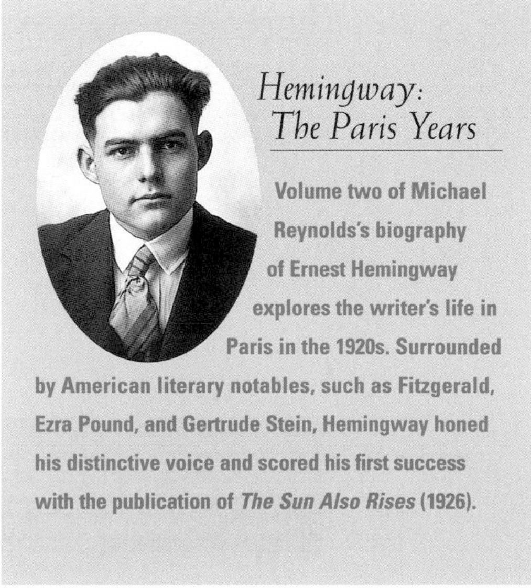

Hemingway: The Paris Years

Volume two of Michael Reynolds's biography of Ernest Hemingway explores the writer's life in Paris in the 1920s. Surrounded by American literary notables, such as Fitzgerald, Ezra Pound, and Gertrude Stein, Hemingway honed his distinctive voice and scored his first success with the publication of *The Sun Also Rises* (1926).

Dorothea Lange: Shooting the Hard Times

A handful of images from the Great Depression have become icons of troubled times and haunted hearts. We see these photographs and no caption is necessary. We know the time. We know the place. Perhaps we can even name the photographer. For this, we can thank Dorothea Lange.

In 1935, with a self-described talent for taking pictures of "people wandering," Lange left a successful portrait business and signed on with the Farm Security Administration (FSA), one of Franklin Roosevelt's programs to revitalize the economy and visually document the nation's social condition. The result was a collection of 270,000 photographs by Lange and others of the farmers and migrant workers who made up a significant portion of the nation's poor during the Depression.

Although her childhood was spent in New York City, far from the fields and conditions she photographed so knowingly, her early years were not without difficulty. She had no father. Her mother worked as a librarian and social worker, exposing Lange to the inner-city plight of tenements and poverty. A childhood bout with polio left one leg shorter and less developed than the other, forcing her to walk with a limp. She took up photography as "a way to maintain myself on the planet."

She ran a successful portrait studio until the start of the Depression in 1930, when compelled by the hardships she saw on her way to work each day—breadlines and strikes—she took her camera into the streets to document what she saw. Even before she began working with the FSA, she amassed enough Depression-era images to organize an exhibition in California in 1934. Although the show received mixed reviews, it attracted the attention of Paul Taylor, a labor economist, who Lange subsequently married. The two worked as a team, producing reports for the FSA that documented the lives of migrant workers. Taylor and Lange tactfully informed the public about the Depression while avoiding rousing public outrage.

Inarguably the most powerful image Lange captured was that of *Migrant Mother,* a downtrodden migrant worker and her three children. The power of that remarkable image has endured for decades. Lange wrote of her exchange with the mother in a California pea-pickers' camp,

> I saw and approached the hungry and desperate mother, as if drawn by a magnet...She told me her age, that she was thirty-two. She said that they had been living on frozen vegetables from the surrounding fields, and birds that the children killed. She had just sold the tires from her car to buy food. There she sat in that lean-to tent with her children huddled around her, and seemed to know that my pictures might help her, and so she helped me. There was a sort of equality about it.
>
> —From DOROTHEA LANGE: A VISUAL LIFE, EDITED BY ELIZABETH PARTRIDGE.

Although her association with the FSA lasted only five years (she was fired for being the "least cooperative" photographer) and was peppered with disagreements about salary, ownership of negatives, and acquiring supplies, Lange was dedicated to the cause and single-mindedly captured the saturated desperation of a vivid time in America's history.

The Oakland Museum of California received an NEH grant to organize and document its Dorthea Lange collection, which includes negative files of more than 25,000 images, over 600 vintage prints, and a selection of Lange's personal papers.

Lange took up photography as "a way to maintain myself on the planet."

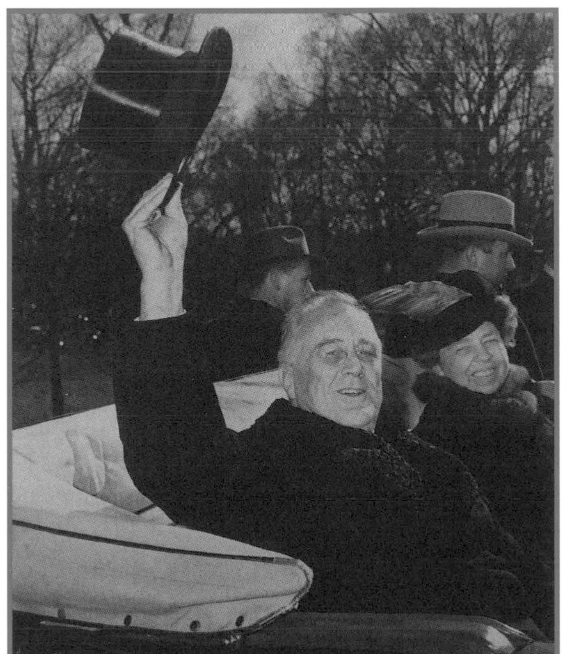

Political Brilliance

More than 15.7 million viewers watched *FDR* when it was first broadcast in 1994. The only four-term president, Franklin Roosevelt led the nation through the Great Depression and World War II. Robert Dallek received the Bancroft Prize for *Franklin D. Roosevelt and American Foreign Policy, 1932–1945.*

Understanding the Great Depression

The New Deal Network (http://newdeal.feri.org/) is a database of more than 20,000 images—photographs, political cartoons, speeches, letters, and other historic documents—many of which were previously accessible only to scholars. Classroom materials help teachers and students understand the Depression. Sponsored by the Franklin and Eleanor Roosevelt Institute, the website is maintained by the Institute for Learning Technologies at Columbia University.

Two Faces of Leadership

A recent spate of movies and books celebrate the role of the citizen soldier in World War II—men who left behind towns big and small for a crew cut, dog tags, and the horror of modern war. But whether they were from Minnesota or New York or Arizona, chances are these soldiers participated in military operations orchestrated by Generals Douglas MacArthur and Dwight Eisenhower.

No two men could have more dissimilar personalities. MacArthur was a brilliant, outspoken soldier with an outsized ego and a healthy contempt for authority; Eisenhower's steady, low-key approach belied his firm, effective leadership skills.

Filmmaker Austin Hoyt has wrestled with the personalities of both men. He served as executive producer for *Eisenhower* and wrote, directed, and produced *MacArthur*. Both films were made with NEH support.

"MacArthur is one of the great figures of the twentieth century," says Hoyt. "He strode across the world stage like Churchill and Roosevelt." During the First World War, MacArthur earned sixteen medals. Afterwards, he served as superintendent at West Point and became Army chief of staff. His rough handling, however, of the Bonus Marchers, World War I veterans demanding pay promised by Congress, drew criticism from President Hoover. Finding him equally volatile, Roosevelt shipped him off to the Philippines. Forced to evacuate the islands after the bombing of Pearl Harbor, MacArthur declared, "I shall return." It took two-and-a-half years, but MacArthur kept his promise.

Chosen to oversee the Japanese surrender, MacArthur conducted the proceedings with dignity. After directing the American occupation of Japan, MacArthur was called once again to field duty with the outbreak of the Korean War. Now seventy years old, he called it "Mars' last gift to an old warrior." MacArthur produced a gift of his own in the successful American landing at Inchon.

MacArthur, however, could not avoid controversy for long. President Truman fired him as commander of the United Nations forces in Korea for openly disputing his policies toward China. Nevertheless, MacArthur returned home a hero and received a ticker tape parade in New York grander than the one for Eisenhower after World War II. In a speech before Congress, he wryly observed that "Old soldiers never die, they just fade away."

Eisenhower fashioned a different sort of career—transitioning from soldier to statesman. The initial assessments of that career by journalists and historians were not kind. He was portrayed as a weak commanding officer and a president inclined to ignore important issues. Eisenhower ignored these judgments, believing history would judge him fairly when the record was known.

The record came to light with the publication of the first volumes of *The Papers of Dwight David Eisenhower*, edited by a team of scholars at Johns Hopkins University with NEH support. The first and greatest misconception dispelled, according to Louis Galanos, professor of history and project editor, was the idea that Eisenhower behaved like a chairman of the board rather than a true wartime commander. Under Eisenhower's direction, the Allies invaded northwest France, launching a campaign that began on the bloody shores of Normandy and ended victorious almost a year later in Berlin. Cables, memos, letters, and diary entries show Eisenhower as a forceful and energetic commander in control of headstrong subordinates such as George Patton and Bernard Law Montgomery.

Later volumes in the series cover the European occupation, his years as Army chief of staff, his terms as president of Columbia University and as Allied commander in Europe for NATO, and the presidency.

Instead of Eisenhower fading away, the publication of his papers produced a sharper picture of the man and fueled a decade-long renaissance in Eisenhower scholarship. Historians now offer an enhanced view of Ike's military leadership and a more generous assessment of his presidential prowess. Rather than being passive, he is portrayed as active and engaged.

Eisenhower was right—he had nothing to worry about.

Produce for Victory

"Produce for Victory," a poster exhibition about the home front during World War II, continues to draw large audiences in small communities across the country. The exhibition, designed for small spaces, was produced by the Smithsonian Institution Traveling Exhibition Service with the assistance of Georgia and four other state humanities councils.

Architect of Recovery

2.2 million people saw ***George Marshall and the American Century***, a ninety-minute documentary about the World War II general, who, as Truman's secretary of state, helped rebuild postwar Europe.

Teaching World War II

Forty schoolteachers studied "The Roosevelt Years: The Depression, the New Deal, and WWII" a four-week summer institute hosted by the Franklin and Eleanor Roosevelt Institute. Forty-five schoolteachers explored "Visions of the Dark Years: Literary and Cinematic Portraits of the German Occupation of France." The five-week summer seminar held in Cannes, France, was sponsored by Texas A&M University.

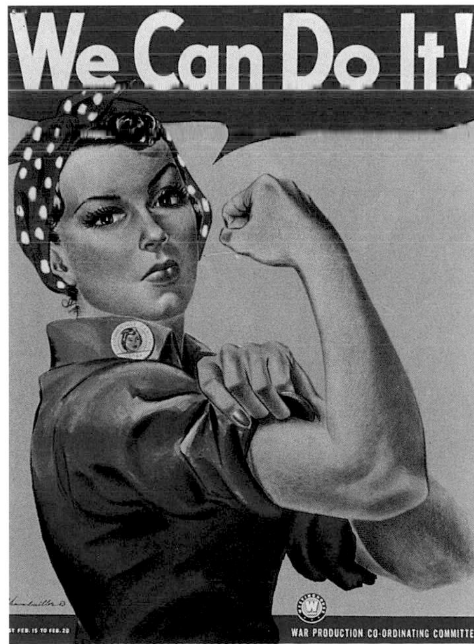

From Rosie to Roosevelt

NEH provided support for "From Rosie to Roosevelt: A Film History of Americans in World War II," a series of six scholar-led, video/reading discussion programs at 120 libraries on the political, military, and social history of America's involvement in World War II.

Capitalism and Its Critic

Nick Salvatore wrote the Bancroft Prize-winning *Eugene V. Debs: Citizen and Socialist.* A tireless labor organizer, Debs ran as the Socialist Party's candidate for U.S. president five times between 1900 and 1920.

Political Flamboyance

Ken Burns's film, *The Life and Times of Huey Long,* uses archival footage and interviews with opponents, allies, and scholars to trace Long's impact on Louisiana politics and the nation.

Rabble-Rousing and Remorse

The political path of Alabama Governor George Wallace brings back riveting images: standing in the school door to bar black students from the University of Alabama in 1963; being gunned down at a shopping mall during a presidential campaign stop in 1972; frail and wheelchair bound in his final years.

In the NEH-supported film, *George Wallace: Settin' the Woods on Fire,* filmmakers Paul Stekler and Daniel McCabe show the ironies of a career that took him from populist to demagogue to penitent.

Wallace got his start as a moderate Democrat. Winning a seat in the Alabama state legislature in 1946, he introduced bills to assist the poor. He asked to be appointed to the board of Tuskegee Institute, the state's most prestigious black university. In the early 1950s, as a circuit court judge, he gained a reputation for demanding that black plaintiffs and lawyers be granted fair treatment.

In 1958, he ran for governor, speaking on behalf of the poor, condemning the Ku Klux Klan, and winning the endorsement of the National Association for the Advancement of Colored People. He lost the election.

With that, Wallace's politics changed. Critics called it Faustian, cynical. Wallace spoke against black voter registration and against integration. He couched his agenda in terms of the federal government intruding into matters better left to state government. In 1962, he was elected governor by a landslide.

Wallace would soon become a national figure as well. In 1963, he stood at the doors of a University of Alabama building to block the entrance of two black students. Three months later, the Ku Klux Klan bombed Birmingham's 16th Street Baptist Church, killing four children. Although bloodshed was not his intent, the nation held him responsible for his fiery words.

Nationally televised beatings of black civil rights activists came soon after. In March 1965, civil rights marchers intended to walk from Selma to the state capital in Montgomery. At the edge of the city, they were met by state troopers wielding sticks, bullwhips, and tear gas. Days later, President Johnson asked Congress to pass the most comprehensive voters' rights bill in history. About Wallace, Richard Jenkins of the *Alabama Journal* notes, "By making an issue of the Civil Rights Act of 1964, and particularly the Voting Rights Act of 1965, his politics and his opposition to the acts, in effect, helped those bills pass."

Wallace made futile runs for the presidency in 1968, 1972, and 1976 while his personal life crumbled around him. His first wife succumbed to cancer. He was confined to a wheelchair after the 1972 shooting. And his second wife divorced him.

After the 1976 defeat, a reflective Wallace called up old enemies to ask forgiveness. The authenticity of his redemption may never be known, but when he ran for governor again in 1982—successfully—he secured the support of black voters and worked closely with them after his election.

Stekler suggests that Wallace's life ends having come full circle: "He begins gifted at politics, an idealist in some ways. He works to become governor but is prevented. He then makes a conscious decision to give up his ideals and embrace racism, gaining more political success and power than he ever believed possible. Then at the height of his power, he is struck down. At the end of his life he returns to his idealism, to his roots."

Mapping Congress

The Historical Atlas of Political Parties in the United States Congress, 1789–1988 **documents the results of every congressional election for each ward, city, county, and state in the United States.**

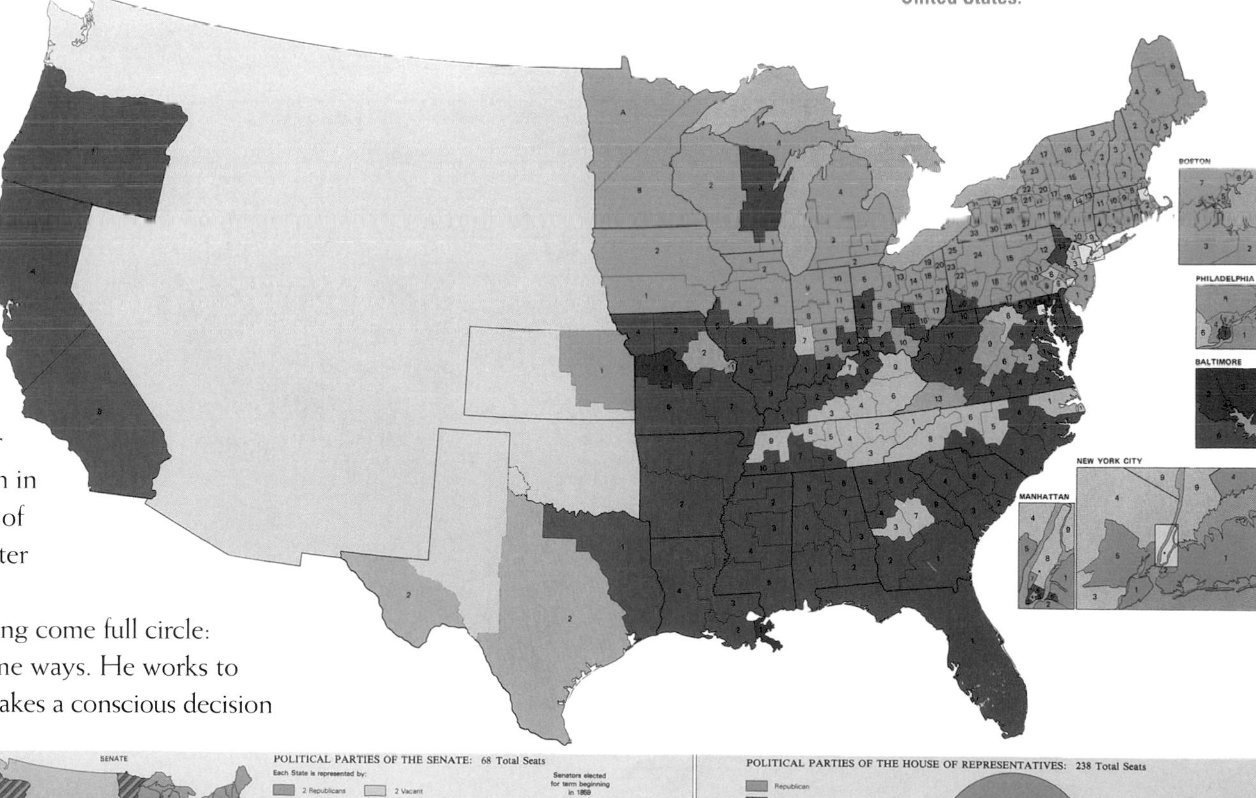

Scientific Thought

NEH supported the creation of *Guided Studies of Great Texts in Science*—authoritative, extensively annotated editions in English of such key works as Ptolemy's *Optics,* Aristotle's writings on biology, Galileo's *Dialogue on the Two Chief World Systems,* Andreas Vesalius's 1543 text on human anatomy, and Newton's *Principia.*

Einstein's State of Motion

The Collected Papers of Albert Einstein—including scientific, professional, and personal papers, manuscripts and correspondence—will fill twenty-five volumes when completed. Seven are available now, with two more in the works.

The Inventive Edison

"I haven't failed. I've just found ten thousand ways that don't work."

In his struggle to succeed—in this case to invent a storage battery—Thomas Edison insisted that persistence was the key. After ten thousand tries, he made a storage battery that functioned. When things worked the first time, he was surprised. One example was the phonograph, as he writes in his lab notes: "It was finished, the foil put on; I then shouted Mary had a little lamb, etc. I adjusted the reproducer and the machine reproduced it perfectly. I was never so taken aback in my life. Everybody was astonished. I was always afraid of things that worked the first time."

The common image of Edison as a solitary genius experiencing isolated inspirations misses the nature of his efforts. He worked with teams of people and meticulously noted his work, leaving behind more than six million pages. With NEH support, scholars at Rutgers University are editing Edison's papers. Half of the microfilming has been completed and three of the projected fifteen volumes have been published.

Members of Edison's team were expected to come up with a set number of ideas each month. At various times, the team included

Henry Ford, who went off to build automobiles, and Lewis Latimer, who invented a workable light bulb before he joined Edison's lab. (His patent, however, came two years later than Edison's.)

Developing the light bulb was a major breakthrough, but Edison also offered an entire concept of lighting. He patented sockets, generators, junction boxes, fuses, mains, conductors, and other components. "My own practice for many years," Edison wrote, "...has been to study a subject for a time, and then taking out patents for such parts of a general system I may succeed in making... As completed they are a system based on different inventions or discoveries, some of which have been made years before the others."

Biographer Paul Israel notes that "Edison possessed a real genius for organizing invention that enabled him to rapidly explore his own ideas and to use the ideas and skills of others to greatest advantage."

In later years, when he cultivated a more solitary image, he became less productive. He failed to grasp the significance of radio and spent more than ten years trying to develop a new way to process iron ore—an enterprise he eventually gave up.

By the time he died in 1931, however, Thomas Edison had been granted 1,093 patents, more than any other person. His record still stands.

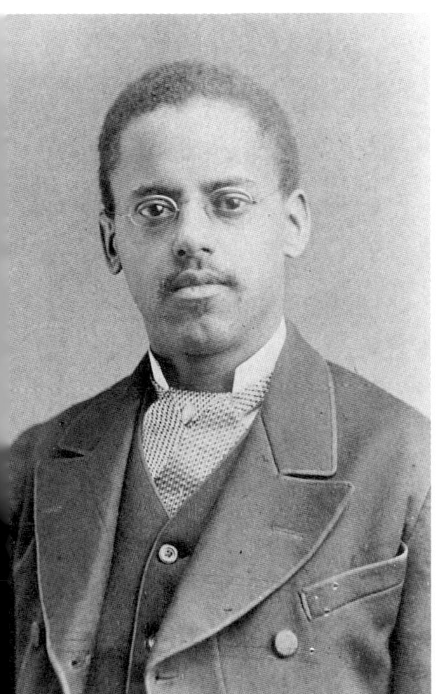

Highlighting Latimer

Queens Borough Public Library in Jamaica, New York, produced "Blueprint for Change: The Life and Times of Lewis H. Latimer," an exhibition and public program about the African American inventor, Lewis Latimer (1848–1928).

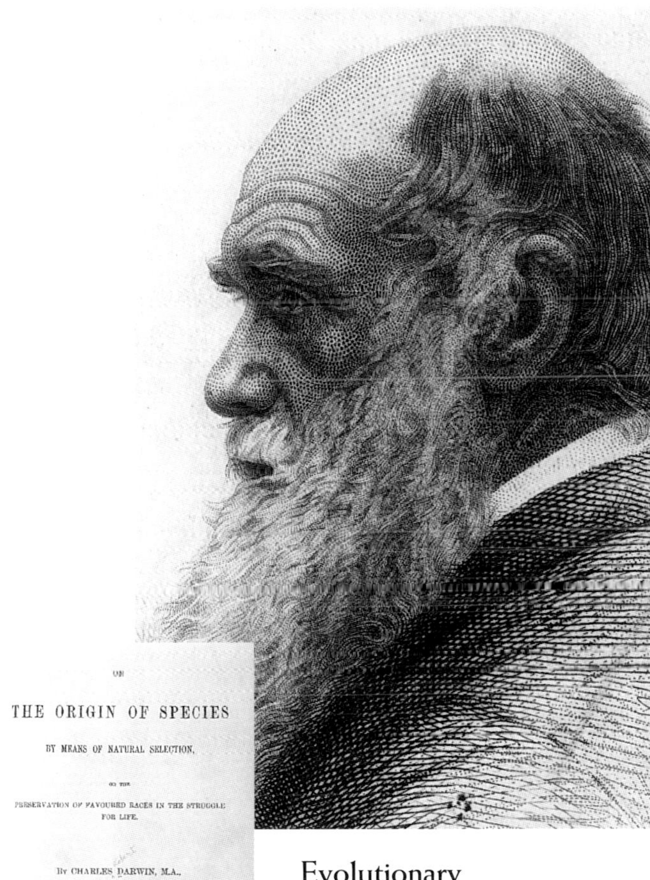

ON
THE ORIGIN OF SPECIES
BY MEANS OF NATURAL SELECTION,
BY CHARLES DARWIN, M.A.
LONDON:
JOHN MURRAY, ALBEMARLE STREET.
1859.

Evolutionary Thinking

The Correspondence of Charles Darwin **shows how a worldwide network of naturalists played a role in refining his theory of natural selection. Editors have collected 9,000 of his letters and 5,000 replies; eleven of the projected thirty-two volumes have been published.**

On the Road

With NEH support, Johns Hopkins University Press printed *The National Road: Theater of American Life* and *A Guide to the National Road: Landscaping and Meaning.*

A Nation on the Move

"O public road...
You express me better than I can express myself"
—Walt Whitman

Poets have written for generations about the restlessness of American life, about an ingredient in the American psyche that keeps people looking beyond the next hill.

A little less than fifty years ago, that restlessness took concrete form in a federal law creating the Interstate Highway System. President Dwight D. Eisenhower pushed for what would become the country's largest public works project, crisscrossing 42,000 miles and altering the physical and cultural landscape forever.

Highways are emblems of our desires, Gertrude Stein says. "Think of anything—of cowboys, of movies, of detective stories, of anybody who goes anywhere—or stays at home—and you will realize that it is something strictly American to conceive a space that is filled with moving. That is filled, always filled, with moving."

Geography professor Karl Raitz adds an academic context: "To know America, therefore, one must understand the development of the road, the access it provides, and the activities it stimulates."

National road-building had its start in 1806 when Congress authorized a National Road to connect the seaports of the east to the remote Northwest Territory. The road brought immigrants to the farmlands of western Pennsylvania, Ohio, Indiana, and Illinois; towns and villages grew up along its edge. Then the advent of railroads and later, the invention of the automobile, changed the landscape.

In 1920, there were eight million cars registered in the United States, by 1940 twenty-seven million, and by 1960 sixty-one million. At that point, three-fourths of all American families owned a car. To millions, it meant the possibility of a new life with a home and yard in the suburbs.

How the face of the country changed is told in *Divided Highways*, a film supported by NEH and the state humanities councils of Texas and Oregon. *Divided Highways* looks at the effects of the interstate system: the towns it opened up to prosperity, the neighborhoods it split, the boom it gave to the steel industry in the 1950s, the car culture it spawned, and the price it paid in oil shortages in the 1970s.

"The highways are divided, and our feelings about them are divided as well," says Larry Hott, producer and director. The film shows the Overland neighborhood of Miami lost in the shadow of I-91, its vacant lots and boarded businesses in stark contrast to the glittering towers of Dallas.

"Dallas was really willed into being by the interstates," says historian of architecture David Dillon. "The interstates have channeled growth; they are the form givers here. They are great public spaces, too. Because they were here first, they haven't devastated the neighborhoods, as they did in Boston or Philadelphia or Chicago. Instead, they spawned enormous amounts of development and have strung the city out in very dramatic ways."

The highways have affected styles of architecture and advertising as well. At highway speed, glass skyscrapers become complementary, offering a reflection of trees and sky at a glance. At ground level, however, the visual din becomes more confusing. Roadside advertising that once featured giant hot dogs and coffee cups has become memorabilia. The signs along the two-lanes have given way to the more abstract and ubiquitous Golden Arches of McDonald's.

My Kind of Town

The Art Institute of Chicago explored the evolution of Chicago's architecture in two traveling exhibitions. The first looked at the built environment of the city at the turn of the century; the second looked at changes before and after the Great Depression and World War II.

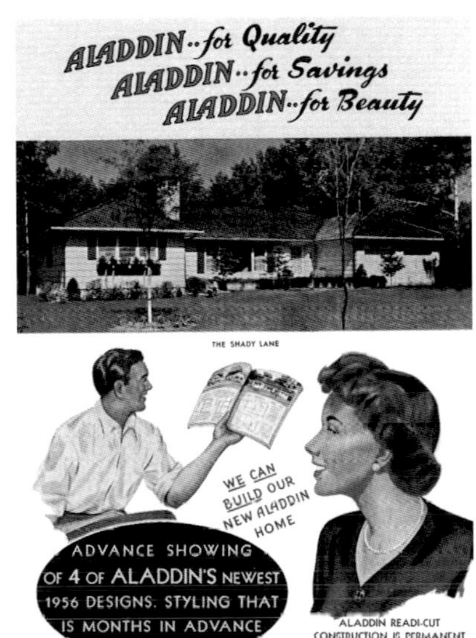

Building the American Dream

From 1906 until 1982, the Aladdin Company provided precut mail-order homes. Its catalogs document the evolution of American vernacular architecture and are housed at the Clarke Historical Library at Central Michigan University.

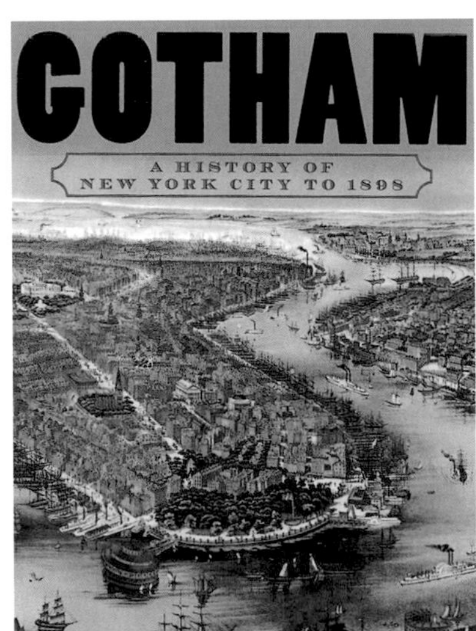

I'll Take Manhattan

How Manhattan Island became one of the world's foremost cities is chronicled in Edwin G. Burrows and Mike Wallace's Pulitzer Prize-winning *Gotham: A History of New York City to 1898* and Ric Burns's ten-hour film, *New York: A Documentary History*.

Ralph Waldo Emerson

An American Landscape

"What appears to be a wild landscape is actually a special kind of cultural landscape that human activity has shaped and continues to shape to the present day," explains Jackie Day, director of the Adirondack Museum in Blue Mountain Lake, New York. In 1999, the museum opened "A Peopled Wilderness," which uses first-person accounts, paintings, photographs, and arts and crafts to illustrate the history of the densely forested region that gained protection as the Adirondack Park in 1892. The exhibition received support from NEH.

In part, the struggle in the 1880s to preserve the park arose from the popular notion of the Adirondacks as wilderness. Literature and art had first fueled people's conceptions of the Adirondacks since early in the century. The publication of James Fenimore Cooper's *The Last of the Mohicans* in 1826 and Charles Fenno Hoffman's *Wild Scenes in the Forest and Prairie* in 1839 popularized the Adirondacks with their tales of adventure. The novels' characters, such as the Adirondack guide Natty Bumpo, set the standard for wilderness folk heroes.

Artists of the Hudson River School, such as Thomas Cole and Asher B. Durand, idealized the landscape and contributed to the Adirondacks' image as a retreat into the beauty of the wilderness. Some painters of this school were opposed to industrialization and sought to conserve the wilderness. "Landscape painters publicized vistas of the Adirondacks that very few people were privy to," says Kenneth Myers, cultural historian and consulting curator at the Adirondack Museum. "They held up the region as an example of the beauty of natural landscape and as an expression of God's approbation of humankind."

The region inspired Ralph Waldo Emerson and other nineteenth-century New England transcendentalists, who believed that divinity permeated nature and all humankind. "In the wilderness we turn to reason and faith," Emerson wrote in his essay, "Nature." Emerson and some of his intellectual circle spent a month fishing and hunting at Follensby Pond in the central Adirondacks. The visit was memorialized in William James Stillman's 1858 painting, "The Philosophers' Camp" and in Emerson's poem, "The Adirondacs."

"Many people think the beauty or meaning of a physical environment is somehow intrinsic or natural," says Myers. "But the meaning we find in places like the Adirondacks is socially constructed and changes all the time.

The Olmstead Papers

Frederick Law Olmstead, the great civic engineer and city planner, transformed a marshy wasteland into New York City's Central Park. Olmstead and other city planners wanted to create a retreat from the closeness of urban life. Scholars at American University prepared an edition of Olmstead's papers.

How we interpret and experience a place changes from generation to generation, as people construct ways of defining the region and themselves."

By the twentieth century, paved roads and the rise of the automobile provided easier access and enabled working and middle-class people to tour inexpensively. The Adirondacks became a vacation spot accessible to everyone.

"Even people who have never been to the Adirondacks have a strong sense of the area as very romantic, very charged, and precious," says Day. "But the story that is not known is the human story of the people who settled the area. We're trying to express their individual voices and show how people valued this place, how they perceived it, and how they used it." ❧

Beyond Walden Pond

An NEH challenge grant helped construct and endow the Thoreau Institute, a research library and archives devoted to the study of the humanities and the environment as it relates to Henry David Thoreau's writings and philosophy. Scholars at the University of California, Santa Barbara, and Northern Illinois University are preparing an authoritative edition of Thoreau's writings.

Henry David Thoreau

Walden Pond

Teaching the Environment

The University of California, Santa Cruz, hosted a five-week summer institute for twenty-five college teachers on "The Environment and World History, 1500–2000." Kansas State University took a more regional approach with "People, Prairies, and Plains: The Historical Role of People in the Environment," a four-week summer institute for thirty schoolteachers.

Jazz

Ken Burns's ten-part film history of *Jazz* traces the genre from Buddy Bolden and Louis Armstrong to Charlie Parker and Wynton Marsalis.

Duke Ellington

"Beyond Category: The Musical Genius of Duke Ellington" traveling exhibition has visited 41 states. The documentary, *Duke Ellington: Reminiscing in Tempo*, traces Ellington's career as a composer and performer.

Preserving Satchmo

The Louis Armstrong House and Archives (www.satchmo.net) contains 650 reel-to-reel tapes, 1,600 commercial recordings, 86 scrapbooks, 5,000 photographs, and a gold-plated trumpet given to Armstrong by the King of England

Marian Anderson Papers

A University of Pennsylvania database (webdb.library.upenn.edu/anderson) holds 360 linear feet of the personal papers of singer Marian Anderson (1897–1993), including scores and recordings.

And All That Jazz

George Gershwin

Two thousand years from now, the writer Gerald Early has said, America will be remembered for three things: the Constitution, baseball, and jazz. "They are the three most beautifully designed things this culture has ever produced."

"A certain kind of paradox is built into jazz music," comments Early, who is a professor of English and head of the African and African American Culture Studies Program at Washington University in St. Louis. "You had people who created a music that's really celebrating democratic possibilities: liberation, freedom of the spirit, a soaring above adversities—who really hadn't experienced everything that democratic society had to offer, but you could look around and see the promise embedded in the society."

"Democratic possibilities." It is a leitmotiv that runs through the history of American music from the earliest militia bands of the American Revolution through Aaron Copland to Duke Ellington and George Gershwin.

"We have been shown the value of music from folk tradition and music from popular traditions and music from classical traditions," says music historian Richard Crawford, "and our passion for preserving the past is so well developed that the biodegradability of music, taken for granted in earlier times, doesn't exist any more. We have more and more music in the present that we have to try to come to terms with."

Part of the job of sorting it out has fallen to Crawford as general editor of *Music of the United States of America* (www.umich.edu/~musausa/index.html), forty scholarly editions on America's music. Completed volumes include Irving Berlin's early popular works and Amy Beach's *Quartet for Strings*, with volumes of Charles Ives's music, John Philip Sousa marches, American fiddle tunes, slave songs, George Gershwin's *Rhapsody in Blue*, and Fats Waller organ performances in the works.

Knowing the Score

Johns Hopkins digitized its Lester S. Levy Sheet Music Collection (http://levysheet music.mse.jhu.edu), which consists of more than twenty-nine thousand pieces of popular American music from 1780 to 1960. The American Music Center, Inc., cataloged eighty-seven hundred scores by contemporary American composers.

American Wars in Asia

The United States fought three wars in Asia during the twentieth century—Japan, Korea, and Vietnam—with mixed results. In the ensuing years, fiction writers and poets on both sides have created a significant body of literature that documents the trauma, explores loss of innocence, and calls for remembrance.

Excerpts from many of these stories and poems will be available online in a digital resource library being developed by the American Wars in Asia Project (www.umt.edu/mansfield/drl/default.htm) at the University of Montana's Mansfield Center. "Our core objective is to promote imaginative ways of looking at international conflict and talking about the experience of war," says Philip West, the project's director. In addition to poetry and fiction, the library's users will eventually be able to access film clips, art, photographs, memoirs, autobiographies, newspaper articles, and government documents.

The project developed from a 1995 NEH summer institute for college and university teachers. A collection of essays stemming from the institute, *American Wars in Asia: A Cultural Approach to History and Memory,* was published in 1998.

After the Second World War, the U.S. forces occupying Japan censored all discussion of the August 1945 atomic bombings at Hiroshima and Nagasaki. Japanese society ostracized the *hibakusha,* the survivors of the bombings, who were often physically marked and regarded as unmarriageable. Nevertheless, Nagai Takashi, a young, widowed father wrote prolifically until his death in 1951, establishing a genre of *hibakusha* literature. "Was not Nagasaki the chosen victim," Nagai wrote in *Bells of Nagasaki,* "the lamb without blemish, slain as a whole-burnt offering on an altar of sacrifice, atoning for the sins of all the nations during World War II?"

American involvement in Korea terrified many Japanese, who feared the possibility of a third world war. In the United States, the unpopular conflict was quickly forgotten. In an essay in *America's Wars in Asia,* David McCann explores why America seemingly "forgot" about Korea. He argues that the literary works of the First World War and the Spanish Civil War ended the rhetorical tradition of portraying death as a "noble sacrifice," and the literary response to World War II tended to deny any overarching significance to death. McCann concludes that America's literary tradition, having dealt with war through irony, silence, and reportage,

The Life and Times of LBJ

During Lyndon Johnson's presidency, American involvement in Vietnam escalated. The four-part documentary *LBJ* traces the political career of the plain-spoken Texan who championed civil rights, offered a vision of a Great Society, and embroiled the country in a controversial war.

formed "a predisposition not to seek literary heroism in connection with the war in Korea."

In Korean literature, the war is often treated as a civil war, whose origins can be found in the struggle against Japanese occupation. The Japanese suppressed Korean stories of social and political upheaval because they were considered anti-imperialist and pro-nationalist. After the country's division, these stories were viewed in South Korea as being sympathetic to the Communists. In North Korea, they were seen as reflecting favorably on Syngman Rhee's government.

Unlike Korea, a great deal has been written about the Vietnam War. The fiction and poetry of Americans and Vietnamese who witnessed the war employ a common approach to style and form. In fiction, a quickly shifting narrative, lack of superstructure, and absence of transitions often disorient and frustrate the reader. "In any war story, it's difficult to separate what happened from what seemed to happen," writes Tim O'Brien in *The Things They Carried*. "What seems to happen becomes its own happening and has to be told that way... The pictures get jumbled; you tend to miss a lot." In a similar vein, Vietnam War poetry is structurally fragmented and often consists of snapshot-like images. Consider Yusef Komunyakaa's description of a girl burning from napalm in "You and I Are Disappearing."

> *We stand with our hands*
> *hanging at our sides,*
> *while she burns*
> *like a sack of dry ice.*
> *She burns like oil on water.*
> *She burns like a cattail torch*
> *dipped in gasoline...*

"By supplementing traditional histories with literature and art," says West, "we're using another lens to look at people and their experiences. We're asking the question, what is the impact of war in human terms?"

The War on Television

With French colonial Indochina as background, the thirteen-part *Vietnam: A Television History* chronicles three decades of conflict in Southeast Asia and its effect on American domestic politics. *Television's Vietnam: Impact of the Media* critiques the above documentary and examines the role of the media in creating perceptions that influenced the course of the war.

A Vietnam Story

Mai Elliott's *The Sacred Willow: Four Generations in the Life of a Vietnamese Family* recounts the political and social choices made by a middle-class family caught in a volatile struggle. Elliott uses her family's story—her great-grandfather was a mandarin and member of the imperial court; her father was a government official under French rule; her older sister married a Communist—as a window into the history of modern Vietnam.

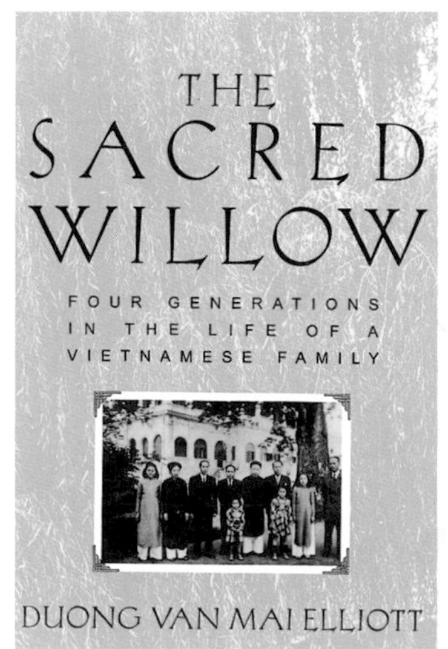

Dictionary of American Regional English

"Everybody is to some extent aware of the differences in regional speech," said Frederick Cassidy, the former editor of the *Dictionary of American Regional English* (DARE). Now in its fourth decade of production, DARE records and describes regional patterns of American English.

Entries are based on a wide variety of sources—regional fiction, diaries, letters, memoirs, histories, travel books, folklore, newspapers, and scholarly literature—but fieldwork done between 1965 and 1970 is of particular importance. In 1,002 communities across the country, eighty fieldworkers interviewed 2,777 people on an extensive range of subjects and made 1,843 recordings of individuals reading a standard text. The recordings, said Cassidy "give the dictionary an accuracy that others don't have. It uses the actual speech of actual people and doesn't rely only on secondhand materials and editors." The fieldwork was vital in preserving the vernacular of what Cassidy called the "horse-and-buggy" generation—a generation and language rapidly dying off. "There is a difference between horse-and-buggy language and the language of automobiles," he said. "DARE shows that there has been a tremendous change in language with the mechanization of society."

Beyond being a source of continual fascination for wordsmiths, DARE also represents a stalwart contribution to linguistic studies. It complements and expands on the existing historical and dialect-focused dictionaries by incorporating maps of regional word distributions into its text.

Since before the turn of the century, American philologists had wanted to create a dictionary to document the richness and diversity of American speech. Spurred by Joseph Wright's *English Dialect Dictionary* (1889), American philologists formed the American Dialect Society, intending to duplicate his effort. Although the society made efforts to collect material, DARE did not take shape until Cassidy was appointed chief editor in 1963. In overseeing the project, Cassidy drew on experience he gained doing fieldwork in Wisconsin for the *Linguistic Atlas of the North Central States* and for his own *Dictionary of Jamaican English*.

From the start, the DARE editors assumed that teachers and librarians would be heavy users, which turned out to be true. But DARE has also proved to be a valuable resource for physicians who need help deciphering folk terms used to describe ailments by their patients; law officers who use it to construct profiles of suspects based on their speech patterns; and historians who use it to make sense of unfamiliar words in seventeenth-century documents. Novelists, poets, folklorists, actors, and directors have also found it helpful.

Since 1970, NEH has supported DARE through outright grants and matching funds. The collection of audiotapes made during fieldwork has also been preserved for use by scholars with NEH support.

When completed, DARE will comprise six volumes. The first three volumes, covering A through O, have been published. The DARE team is currently at work on volume four, which contains P, Q, R, and part of S. The sixth volume will contain a bibliography of sources, a complete list of all the responses garnered from the field questionnaire, and cumulative indices. Sadly, Cassidy did not live to see the completion of DARE; he passed away at the age of 92 in June 2000.

Shelby Foote

Eudora Welty

Southern Stories

The film, *Tell About the South,* charts the parallel histories of African American and white Southern literature and explores the regional uniqueness of the South. It features the work of William Faulkner, Zora Neale Hurston, and Flannery O'Connor, along with interviews with writers Alice Walker, William Styron, Shelby Foote, and Eudora Welty.

Inventing the Middle West

The University of Wisconsin's Elvehjem Museum of Art created the exhibition "John Steuart Curry: Inventing the Middle West." Painting in the first half of the twentieth century, Curry (1897–1946) became a nationally acclaimed champion of America's rural and small-town life and chronicled its Depression-era myths, realities, and ideals.

Defining a Place

Encyclopedia of Indianapolis
Indiana University

The Encyclopedia of Chicago History
Newberry Library and Chicago Historical Society

The Encyclopedia of New England
University of New Hampshire

The Encyclopedia of New York
New York Historical Society

The Encyclopedia of Southern Culture
University of Mississippi

The Encyclopedia of the Great Plains
University of Nebraska

The Handbook of Texas
Texas State Historical Association

Regional Centers

"One place comprehended can make us understand other places better," wrote Eudora Welty. "Sense of place gives us equilibrium; extended, it is sense of direction too." In 1999, NEH launched an initiative to support the creation of ten regional humanities centers where American cultures and traditions can be explored in the context of place. Through this initiative, NEH seeks to provide venues for the exploration of a region's history, its people, its diverse cultural expressions, and its symbolic and physical environment. The centers will serve as hubs for supporting research on regional topics; for documenting and preserving regional history and cultural resources; for developing K–12, undergraduate, and graduate-level educational programs; for designing programming to develop and engage public audiences; and for developing resources for cultural heritage tourism.

Teaching Writing

In 1974, the Bay Area Writing Project was formed to address concerns about student writing skills at all levels of education. With NEH support, the project evolved into the National Writing Project, which is dedicated to training teachers to teach writing. The project recently received its own line in the Department of Education's budget.

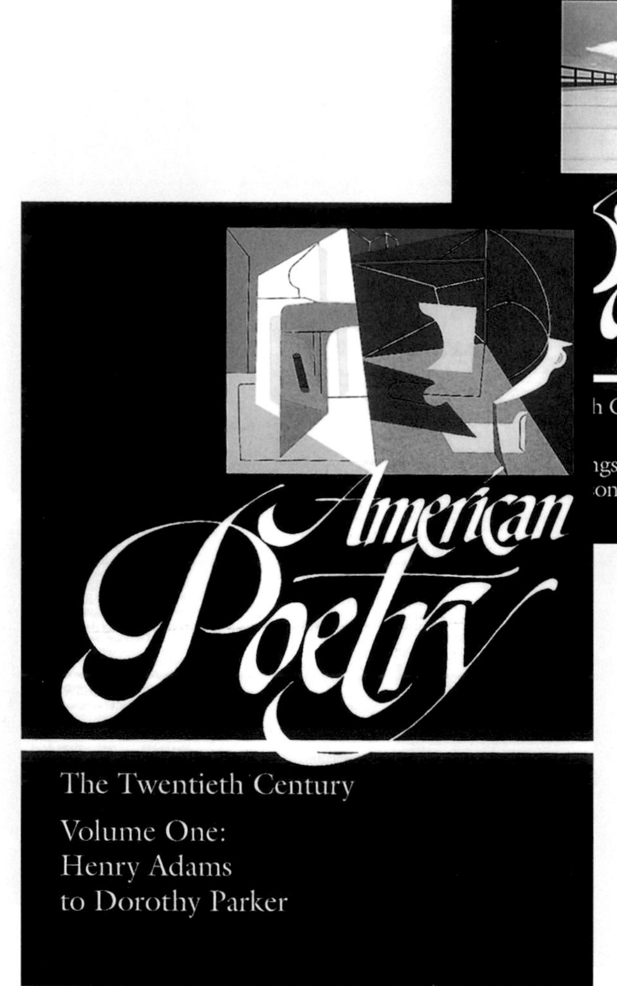

American
Poetry
The Twentieth Century
Volume One:
Henry Adams
to Dorothy Parker

The Library of America

For more than twenty years, the Library of America has preserved the nation's literary heritage by publishing editions of significant works by America's foremost novelists, historians, poets, essayists, political figures, and philosophers.

Founded in 1979 with support from NEH and the Ford Foundation, the Library of America has published 116 volumes to date. "Our image has changed slightly over the years," says Cheryl Hurley, its president. "We had been known as a quality nonprofit publisher. Now people see us as a cultural institution, as a preservation organization keeping these important works in print."

The idea for the Library of America grew out of a concern by scholars and literary critics that many works by America's finest writers were out of print or difficult to find. The series, however, is "not just what you read in high school," says Hurley. "It is broader and deeper, and we are far from exhausting our literary heritage."

Published in hardcover and priced to be affordable, the series covers the range of American writing from Thomas Jefferson, Walt Whitman, and Ralph Waldo Emerson to Willa Cather, Robert Frost, and James Baldwin. Each volume includes a chronology of the author's life and work, helpful notes prepared by a leading expert in the field, and a brief essay about the text.

The Library of America has also made a commitment to providing an authoritative edition of each work. It investigates the work's publishing and printing history, recapturing passages that might have been altered over the years. One such investigation resulted in the restoration of passages from Richard Wright's *Native Son* that were omitted or changed because of their sexual, racial, or political candor.

The newest entry in the series is the two-volume *American Poetry: The Twentieth Century*. The anthology is, says Hurley, "almost bursting at the seams with modern American poetry." The volumes take the reader

The Sound of Poetry

One million Americans use cassettes from the NEH-supported *Voices and Visions* series on poets. As a telecourse, *Voices* reached more than 200 colleges, 2,000 high schools, and 500 public libraries.

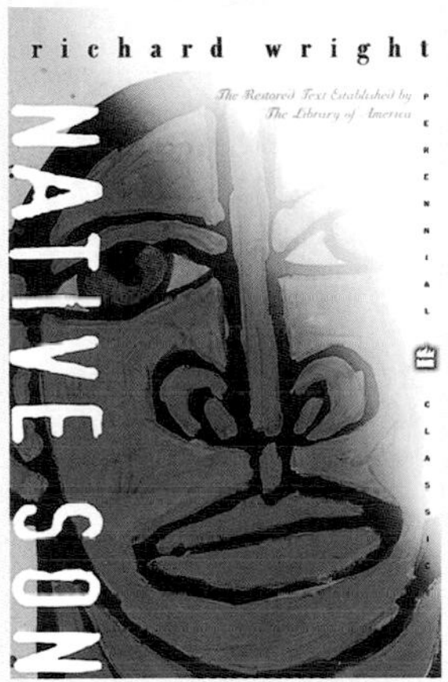

from Henry Adams (1838–1918) to Mary Swenson (1913–1989). Included are Robert Frost, Wallace Stevens, Marianne Moore, T.S. Eliot, and Langston Hughes, as well as less famous writers, such as Witter Bynner, Mina Loy, and Louis Zukofsky. *American Poetry* also includes the witticisms of Ogden Nash and Dorothy Parker, the blues lines of Ma Rainey and Robert Johnson, and the lyrics of George Gershwin and Cole Porter. Some of the material has never been reprinted before.

New editions include: a book of writings about the sea, the early novels of F. Scott Fitzgerald, the plays of Tennessee Williams, and the poetry of Henry Wadsworth Longfellow.

"We want to give the general reader an ample selection," says Hurley. "If all the books in the world disappeared except for the Library of America, a reader would have enough of each American writer to get the full flavor of our rich literary heritage."

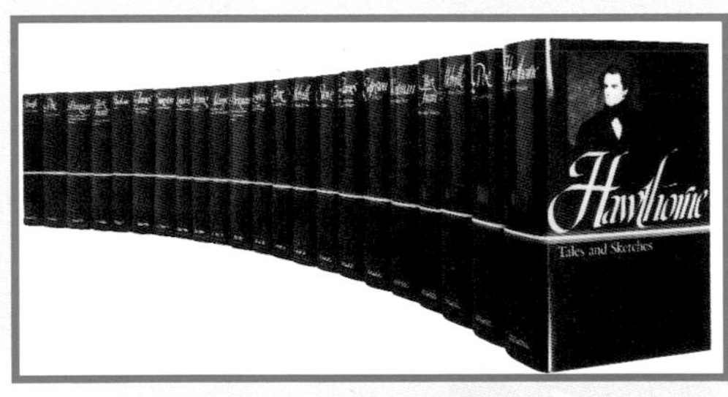

Putting Books on Library Shelves

Eight hundred of the nation's smallest libraries will benefit from a $1 million grant by the Carnegie Corporation to NEH, in which the Endowment will work with the Library of America and the American Library Association to provide the Library of America's fifty most recent titles.

Book Discussion Programs

In the early 1980s, the American Library Association, with support from NEH, developed "Let's Talk About It." This highly successful reading and discussion program brings together scholars and interested readers to discuss thematically related books. Over the past fifteen years, "Let's Talk About It," has been used by hundreds of libraries nationwide. NEH recently awarded grants to forty libraries for "Let's Talk About It.: The Next Generation."

Book Festivals Supported or Conducted by State Humanities Councils

Arizona Book Festival

Baltimore Book Festival (Maryland)

Great Basin Book Festival (Nevada)

Great Illinois Book Fair

Great Salt Lake Book Festival (Utah)

The Montana Festival of the Book

North Carolina Literary Festival

Northwest Bookfest (Washington)

Rocky Mountain Book Festival (Colorado)

South Carolina Book Festival

Southern Festival of Books (Tennessee)

Texas Book Festival

Virginia Festival of the Book

Making the Medieval Accessible

The most complete account of the exploits of King Arthur and the Knights of the Roundtable can be found in five interrelated thirteenth-century French narratives. With NEH support, scholars at Indiana University-Bloomington translated the texts into English. Another team of scholars at Indiana developed *Thesaurus Musicarum Latinarum*, a database of the entire body of Latin music theory written during the Middle Ages and the early Renaissance.

Medieval Illumination

The Middle Ages. The term conjures up images of King Arthur, fair maidens, and the plague. But, what was *middle* about them? "We talk about the Middle Ages because the Renaissance humanists thought of a middle age that came between them and classical antiquity," says Caroline Walker Bynum, who was named the 1999 Jefferson Lecturer for her pathbreaking scholarship on the relationship between women and religion in the Middle Ages. Her work, which takes an interdisciplinary approach to the period, reflects a general trend in medieval scholarship over the past three decades.

Traditionally, the Middle Ages were viewed as historically significant because of institutional, political, and constitutional developments. The period laid the structural foundation for the modern world and much of what has come to be known as the Western Tradition. It contains not only the roots of the British and American legal systems, but also the origins of the modern university. "We do not actually understand modern constitutional government if we do not understand the central and later Middle Ages," observes Bynum.

In recent years, however, scholars have been asking questions about how the Middle Ages differed from the modern world. The shift in emphasis comes from the use of anthropological methods rather than political science models. The change in approach provided new avenues of research, refined previous findings, and heightened the contrast between the medieval and modern periods. "The Middle Ages in many ways is not like the modern world," says Bynum. "I think understanding this is just as useful because it gives you a built-in contrast within your own tradition. The only way to understand yourself or your own society is by seeing how it might be other. Where some things are familiar, the differences stand out more starkly."

Anthropology and literary theory provided medievalists with new tools a decade ago, but technology promises to push out the limits of the field once again.

One cutting-edge project is changing the very text of *Beowulf*. Considered to be the seminal achievement of Old English literature and the earliest European epic written in the vernacular, the poem tells the story of Beowulf, a young prince, and his struggle with the evil monster Grendel. The Electronic Beowulf Project at the University of Kentucky is using fiber optics and ultraviolet light to illuminate the only surviving *Beowulf* manuscript. The process has recovered pieces of the text lost through well-intentioned, but ultimately destructive, nineteenth-century

preservation efforts and uncovered scores of "corrections" made by the scribes who wrote the legend down.

Technology is illuminating other manuscripts too. The Middle English Texts Series, or METS project, is expanding the canon by making obscure and out-of-print works available in durable, reasonably priced scholarly editions and on the Internet. Previously, the study of medieval English literature focused on a canon of core authors: Chaucer, the Gawain-Poet, Langland, and Malory. Now, however, more than one hundred texts are online at the METS website (www.lib.rochester.edu/camelot/teams/tmsmenu.htm), complete with scholarly essays and linked annotations for easy navigation between text and notes.

The series includes the only student editions in Middle English of *The Book of Margery Kempe* and Gallacher's *The Cloud of Unknowing*, a key text about medieval English mysticism; medieval English political writings; the first scholarly publication of the *Middle English Breton Lays*; and the definitive volume of *Robin Hood* and other outlaw tales.

As technology continues to enhance the corpus and possibilities of medieval scholarship, new interpretations are sure to follow. But refining the story is, after all, what scholars do. As Bynum observes in *Fragmentation and Redemption*, "I suggest that the pleasure we find in research and story-telling about the past is enhanced both by awareness that our own voices are provisional and by confidence in the revisions the future will bring."

Telling Chaucer's Tales

Scholars at the University of Rochester are assembling a sixteen-volume series of annotated bibliographies on all significant material published in the twentieth century about *Canterbury Tales* author, Geoffrey Chaucer.

The Cathedral as Text

More than 120 schoolteachers have participated in summer seminars that study Gothic cathedrals as a way of understanding medieval society. During onsite explorations of Notre Dame, St. Denis, and Chartres, the teachers explored religious practices, building techniques, and the role of patronage in medieval culture. The seminars were sponsored by Cornell University.

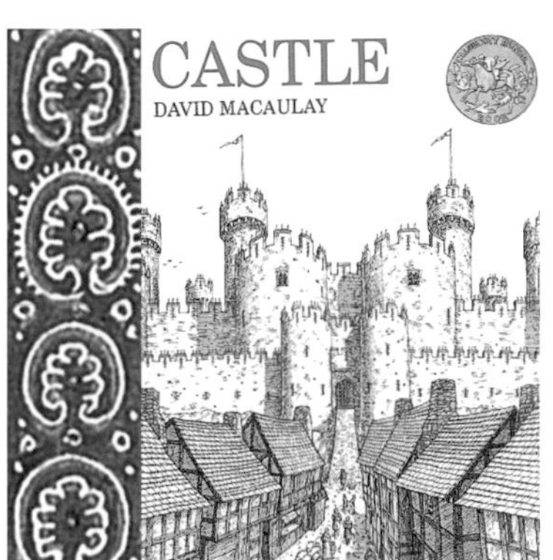

Building Castles and Cathedrals

Two films based on books by David Macaulay explore the architectural achievements of the Middle Ages. *Castle* explains the architectural design, social organization, and military significance of a thirteenth-century Welsh castle, and *Cathedral* tells the story of the planning, construction, and dedication of a fictional cathedral in medieval France.

The Many Realms of King Arthur

Two million Americans visited "The Many Realms of King Arthur." The traveling exhibition was the focal point for reading-and-discussion groups at more than sixty libraries, in conjunction with books about the Arthurian legend: T.H. White's *The Once and Future King*, Tennyson's *Idylls of the King*, and others. The exhibition was created by the Newberry and New York Public Libraries and designed for travel by the American Library Association.

MR. WILLIAM
SHAKESPEARES
COMEDIES,
HISTORIES, &
TRAGEDIES.
Publiſhed according to the True Originall Copies.

LONDON
Printed by Iſaac Iaggard, and Ed. Blount. 1623.

AN
EXCELLENT
conceited Tragedie
OF
Romeo and Iuliet.
As it hath been often (with great applause) plaid publiquely, by the right Honourable the L. of Hunsdon his Seruants.

LONDON,
Printed by Iohn Danter.
1597

A
Midſommer nights
dreame.
As it hath beene ſundry times publickely acted, by the Right honourable, the Lord Chamberlaine his ſeruants.
Written by William Shakeſpeare.

Imprinted at London, for Thomas Fisher, and are to be soulde at his shoppe, at the Signe of the White Hart, in Fleetestreete. 1600.

Shakespeare in the Classroom

William Shakespeare "was not of an age, but for all time" observed Ben Jonson. This claim has been borne out by the enduring popularity of Shakespeare's plays. Considered England's greatest national poet, Shakespeare is the most commonly taught author in American classrooms. The lessons his plays offer on values, heroism, and human frailty continue to engage students and teachers, but they do not always make for easy reading. The quirks of sixteenth-century English can be a formidable obstacle when following Shakespeare's plot twists. Teachers are always looking for fresh approaches to Shakespeare's work—ways to help their students identify with characters and be swept away by grand moments, even when couched in rhyming couplets.

Hundreds of teachers have discovered such innovative methods at NEH summer seminars and institutes. Each year, teachers from across the nation meet with scholars for four to six weeks at colleges, universities, and libraries to explore significant humanities themes, texts, and topics. American teachers have benefited from more than eighty summer seminars and institutes on Shakespeare—more than on any other subject.

NEH funded its first seminar and institutes for college teachers in 1973 and expanded the program in 1982 to include schoolteachers. The idea behind the program was that teachers needed to have an opportunity to be students again—to remember what it is like to learn and explore. The experience reinvigorates their classroom teaching by promoting links between teaching and research; deepening knowledge and understanding of the subject; enhancing the intellectual vitality and professional development of teachers; and providing models of scholarship and teaching.

Two long-running summer seminar programs on Shakespeare are hosted by the Folger Shakespeare Library in Washington, D.C., and by Southern Oregon University. The Folger, a private research library housing the largest extant collection of materials pertaining to Shakespeare and the Renaissance, is also an international center for Shakespeare education. During the summer, the Folger brings together teachers from across the country at its Teaching Shakespeare Institute. The "Shakespeare in Ashland" program hosted by Southern Oregon University coincides with the annual Ashland Shakespeare Festival. Although drawing on different resources, both programs emphasize critical analysis, historical scholarship, and classroom-based performance as tools for teaching Shakespeare. They believe that active learning—

speaking the lines that Will wrote and allowing students to make their own connections to the plays—provides the keys to understanding and enjoying Shakespeare.

Other institutions have hosted Shakespeare programs as well:

Shakespeare & Company of Lenox, Massachusetts, conducted a three-year project on Shakespeare involving institutes, workshops, and curriculum development for Boston elementary and secondary schoolteachers.

The University of Arizona directed the five-week Arizona Shakespeare-Milton Institute. Ninety secondary schoolteachers studied five plays by Shakespeare and Milton's *Paradise Lost.*

The University of Maryland hosted a three-year program of seminars, summer institutes, lectures, workshops, and annual conferences for 1,300 Maryland secondary schoolteachers on Shakespeare and American literature.

The results of seminars and institutes like these are "big and important" according to Peggy O'Brien, who, as director of education at the Folger, pioneered the library's summer seminars. "Real and active familiarity with Shakespeare or any piece of classical literature—and the language of ideas, plots, and characters that they give us," she has written, "creates an intellectual experience that our students are worthy of and a power of investment that all students deserve."

Authoritative Editions

NEH supported the preparation of variorum editions of *Hamlet, All's Well That Ends Well, A Winter's Tale,* and *Coriolanus.* The new editions include the full range of the play's interpretations, textual variants, stage history, and adaptations.

The Shakespeare Hour

***The Shakespeare Hour* combines key moments from five plays originally performed by the BBC, with short introductions, historical background, and commentary from Shakespeare scholars. The five hour-long segments on *A Midsummer Night's Dream, Twelfth Night, All's Well That Ends Well, Measure for Measure,* and *King Lear* are narrated by Walter Matthau.**

Researching the Era of the Bard

Residential fellowships at the Folger Shakespeare Library allow scholars to spend six to nine months using the library's more than 300,000 books and manuscripts on British and European literary, cultural, political, religious, and social history from the fifteenth through the eighteenth centuries.

Translating Culture

In the late 1550s, the keepers of the *Popul Vuh,* the Quiché Mayan book of creation, used the Roman alphabet to record a story that had for centuries been told in Mayan hieroglyphics. It spoke of the deeds of the Mayan gods who dwelled in the darkness of a primordial sea and celebrated the founding of the Quiché kingdom in the Guatemalan highlands.

Because of the insights it provides into ancient Mayan mythology and culture, *Popul Vuh: The Mayan Book of the Dawn of Life* is considered to be one of the most important texts written in the native languages of the Americas. At the core of the story is the relationship between myth and history that reflects the duality of Quiché culture: Gods create humans, while humans search for godlike moments in their own lives. The balance between the divine and human is striking. Its equivalent would have been a Hebrew Old Testament with one-half devoted to events preceding Adam and Eve or the Egyptian *Book of the Dead* with a second part detailing the deeds of the living.

The men who wrote down *Popul Vuh* feared the evaporation of their religious ways in the face of Spain's growing power. "We shall bring it out because there is no longer a place to see it," they wrote, referring to the burning of hundreds of hieroglyphic texts by Spanish missionaries. Ironically, Quiché use of the Roman alphabet—a tool of their conquerors—ensured the survival of the defining story of their culture. Dennis Tedlock, a professor of English and anthropology at the State University of New York at Buffalo, created an English-language translation by researching written records and Mayan artwork and hieroglyphics. He received the 1986 PEN Translation Prize for Poetry for his efforts.

Translation of texts opens the door to cultural worlds that would otherwise remain closed to those without extensive language training. Another translation brings to life late nineteenth-century Russian ideas about faith, evil, and freedom. Richard Pevear and Larissa Volokhonsky's dramatic new translation of Fyodor Dostoevsky's *The Brothers Karamazov* pulls the reader into this black comedy of murder, family dysfunction, and social injustice. Pevear and Volokhonsky also received an award from PEN, which praised their work as "a supremely inventive translation… a remarkable act of cultural restoration that is closer to the Russian text than any previous English translation."

With NEH support, scholars have translated more than one thousand works from more than one hundred languages—including Catalan,

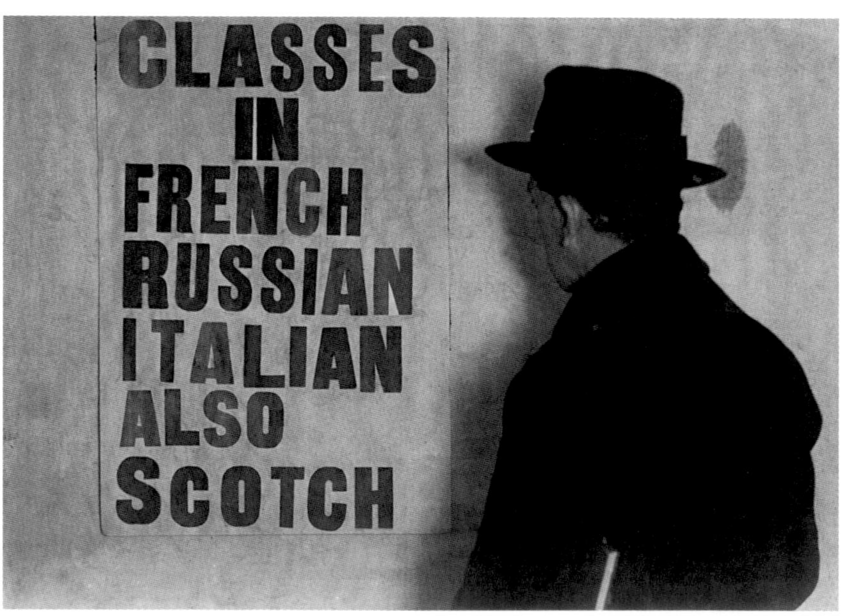

Bengali, Hindi, Armenian, Burmese, Javanese, Malay, Mongolian, and Gaelic—making them accessible to American scholars, teachers, students, and the public.

Translation projects allow Americans to experience other cultures, but they have also been shedding light on the early history of this country. A team of scholars is translating the seventeenth-century records of the colonial government of New Netherland. Written in an archaic form of Dutch, the records continue to be of legal and historical importance for parts of New England and the Middle Atlantic states. Some materials have been incorporated into curricular materials for the fourth and seventh grades. The project has also established an Internet program between schools in Friesland in the Netherlands, and Bethlehem Middle School in New York.

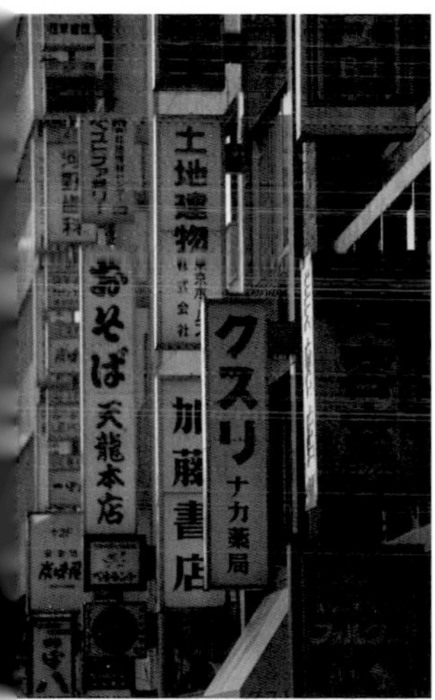

Japanese Language Instruction

NEH has supported initiatives to strengthen foreign language instruction at pre-collegiate and undergraduate levels. Some of the most successful programs have been in Japanese language instruction. Since 1990, the Endowment has awarded numerous grants to the Eugene and Portland, Oregon, public schools to develop Japanese language and cultural immersion programs for grades K–12. The University of Oregon in Eugene received additional funding to develop a national network of Japanese language immersion teachers in elementary schools. The network is still active, and now includes Japanese immersion programs in Cincinnati, Anchorage, Detroit, Charlotte, Portland, Eugene, and several locations in California. An NEH grant to the College Board supported the development of a national achievement test in Japanese. The Massachusetts Institute of Technology developed *Tanabata: The Star Festival,* an interactive video for intermediate instruction in Japanese language and culture; and the Georgia Public Telecommunications Commission designed *Virtual Japan,* an interactive web and CD-ROM-based simulation for teaching Japanese language and culture. The University of North Carolina, Chapel Hill, is now using a certification curriculum developed with NEH funding to train K–12 Japanese language teachers.

Look It Up

The term "dictionary" has expanded in the digital age as scholars take advantage of new technologies, particularly the powerful search and storage possibilities offered by databases.

Dictionary of Old English—*Based upon historical records written between 600 and 1150.*

A Comprehensive Aramaic Lexicon—*Covers texts written from 925 B.C. to A.D. 1400 in Aramaic, the language of Babylonian merchants and portions of the Old Testament.*

The Chicago Hittite Dictionary—*Hittite is the earliest written Indo-European language.*

Historical Dictionary of American Slang—*Charts American colloquial usage from the eighteenth century to the present.*

An Etymological Dictionary of Old High German—*Based on the language used in German literary texts from 750 to 1150.*

A Dictionary of the Aluku (Boni) Language—*Aluku is spoken by the descendants of escaped Dutch slaves in Suriname and French Guiana.*

Sino-Tibetan Etymological Dictionary and Thesaurus—*Documents the lexicographic and etymological origins of the entire family of Sino-Tibetan languages.*

The Chicago Assyrian Dictionary—*Provides a lexicon for Akkadian, the earliest known Semitic language.*

Tsafiqui Ethnolinguistic Database—*The Tsachila people are an indigenous tribe of northwest Ecuador.*

A Khmer Etymological Lexicon—*Khmer is a Cambodian language in the Mon-Khmer family.*

Pennsylvania Sumerian Dictionary—*Sumerian is the oldest known language to be preserved in written form.*

Hittite Sphinx

The Dead Sea Scrolls

One afternoon in 1947, three Bedouin shepherds were herding their flocks on the northwest shore of the Dead Sea near Wadi Qumran. One tossed a rock into a cave opening; they heard something break. Returning later, they entered the cave and discovered ten large pottery jars, one containing three scrolls wrapped in linen. There were still more to be found.

Their discovery was the largest and most significant collection of manuscripts ever uncovered in Palestine. The Dead Sea Scrolls, as they have come to be known, consist of biblical manuscripts and other religious writings dating from 225 B.C. to A.D. 68. Included in the find were texts of Leviticus, Psalms, the oldest witnesses to the Hebrew, Aramaic, and Greek texts of Jewish scripture, along with nonbiblical manuscripts from the destruction of the Second Temple and the time of Christ. Before this discovery, the oldest extensive Hebrew manuscripts of the Old Testament dated from the end of the ninth century A.D. The Dead Sea Scrolls antedated these by a millennium.

The singularity of the texts inspired one of the most protracted and painstaking endeavors of contemporary scholarship. Although the first scrolls found were in good condition, most were not. Some were scraps: an estimated eight hundred manuscripts scattered in 800,000 fragments. Without the protection of pottery jars and linen coverings, the manuscripts were subject to the deteriorating forces of time and nature.

Scholars were faced with the challenge of piecing together the bits, interpreting them, publishing the works, and preserving the originals. An international team took on the task, conducting pioneering work in the fields of paleography, orthography, and archaeology.

The task at hand was to identify and categorize the fragments, differentiate the manuscripts as they were pieced together, and decipher and transcribe the fragments for publication of the *editio princeps*, the first critical edition of the text. The work was done arduously by hand, until a second generation of scholars began producing electronic versions in the mid-1980s. Using these electronic versions, the editors could analyze the

Jews and Judaism

The nine-part documentary series, *Heritage: Civilization and the Jews*, chronicles the 3,000-year history of the Jewish people from their exodus from Egypt to the creation of Israel, the country's early history, and its relationship with Jews worldwide. The series won an Emmy.

texts and assess their relationship to other texts and to ancient translations. Questions, variants, and corrections could be logged more easily and fixed much more quickly.

Since 1986, NEH has supported the publication of the scrolls under the direction of Eugene Ulrich and James Vander Kam, both of the Department of Theology, University of Notre Dame. Twelve of the sixteen volumes of the main corpus of scrolls have been published as part of the *Discoveries in the Judaean Desert* series. The final four volumes are currently in production.

In the years since their discovery, the scrolls have further discolored and deteriorated despite efforts at conservation. Today, scholars use photographs of the text for their studies, but even when photographed with exacting care, many of the scroll texts remain undecipherable.

Scholars and photography experts at the Ancient Biblical Manuscript Center in Claremont, California, devised a method of reading the texts through digital imaging. Photographs are digitized and the digital images are enhanced so that words—obscured by dirt or flaws in the skins on which the texts were written—become visible. With NEH grants, the center has also prepared a database inventory of the fragments and developed standards for digitization. The center's findings are disseminated to repositories of ancient materials throughout the world.

Ice Maiden of the Andes

Johan Reinhard's discovery in Peru of the five-hundred-year-old frozen Inca mummy, the Ice Maiden, was hailed by *TIME* magazine as one of the ten most important scientific discoveries of 1995. Nearly 100,000 people visited the Ice Maiden exhibition in less than one month when it was in the United States for scientific examinations. Reinhard, supported by an NEH fellowship, was researching a book on the role of sacred landscape in Andean cultures when he made the discovery.

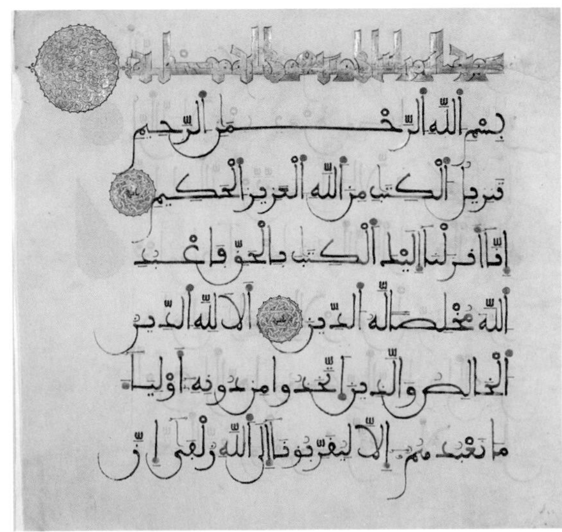

The World of Islam

NEH supported the revision, expansion, and updating of the *Encyclopedia of Islam*, first published in 1908. The new edition, which features articles written by an international team of scholars, has come to define the field and serve as a standard reference. *The World of Islam*, a thirteen-part series of radio documentaries recorded on location in fifteen Muslim countries, explores Islam as a faith, culture, and political ideology.

Translating Buddhism

Key texts of Buddhism have been translated into English, including a sixth-century Chinese manual of Buddhist meditations that influenced Buddhist practices throughout East Asia; a seventh-century classical Sanskrit text, regarded as the definitive statement of the epistemological and logical doctrines of Buddhism; and *The Essentials of Ch'an*, a collection of works on Zen Buddhism written by a thirteenth-century Chinese monk.

Home Away from Home

Three American institutions in the Middle East—the W.F. Albright Institute of Archaeological Research in Jerusalem, American Center of Oriental Research in Jordan, and American Research Center in Egypt—have used NEH challenge grants to improve their facilities and provide support for researchers. In addition to serving as a home base, the centers help American scholars obtain clearances from local governments to conduct research.

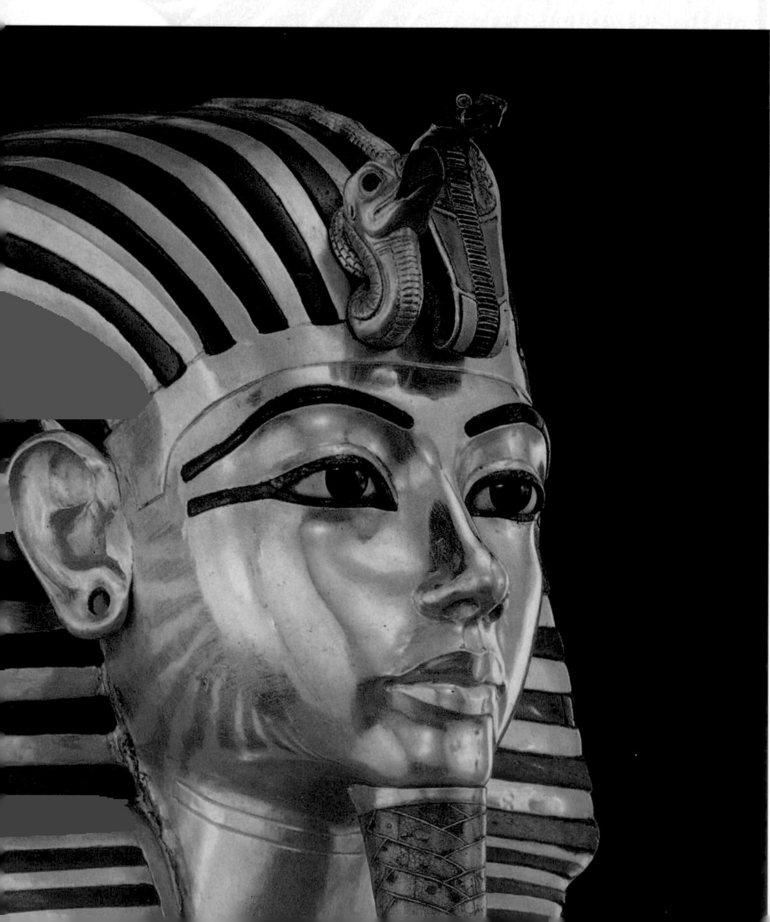

The Magnificence of Tut

Of the hundreds of tombs created to honor kings during Egypt's Golden Age, the legendary tombs of Tutankhamen was one of the few to be discovered largely intact. When, in 1922, British archaeologist Howard Carter uncovered the tomb of Tutankhamen with its thousands of treasures, he made one of the greatest archaeological finds in history. And when those treasures came to America in "Treasures of Tutankhamen," they became the greatest museum draw of the time, attracting more than one million people to the Metropolitan Museum of Art in New York and hundreds of thousands more in Chicago, New Orleans, Washington, D.C., and Seattle in 1978 and 1979.

"Tutankhamen was a turning point in museum-going," says Kathleen Orffmann, who, as manager of visitor services at the Metropolitan, devised the dated-and-timed ticket concept for the exhibition. "After Tutankhamen, people became permanently interested in museum events."

The fifty-five objects comprising the exhibition were carefully selected from the five thousand originally excavated: alabaster cups, gold sculptures of Tutankhamen, furniture, and jewelry. The exhibition's major object, and the tomb's most famous find, is Tutankhamen's solid gold mask, found in place over the mummy's head and shoulders.

Besides being fascinated with the objects, museum-goers were enthralled by the stories of the young king's life and of the archaeological discovery and excavation of the tomb. The National Gallery of Art in Washington, D.C., recreated the tomb for visitors, enhanced with photomurals and wall captions from Carter's three-volume journal of the expedition.

While the exhibition planners knew it would be a blockbuster, they never dreamed it would attract the huge crowds it did. According to Orffmann, the exhibition was the largest-selling event of any kind—including concerts and sports events—in the history of computerized ticketing.

"The exhibition sold 900,000 tickets in five days," she says of its New York stay. What brought out so many to a museum exhibition? Orffmann says there were a number of reasons.

"There is a fascination with the subject—Egypt and early civilization and with mummies," she says, noting that the Metropolitan's permanent exhibition is second only to European paintings in popularity. "There was also interest in seeing the objects made of gold, and in knowing it was the greatest archaeological find in history."

When the exhibition closed, its contents were returned to Egypt where they are now on display at the Egyptian Museum in Cairo. A survey by the Metropolitan showed that twenty-nine percent of those visiting the King Tutankhamen exhibition were first-time museum visitors.

"That 29 percent were introduced to museum-going and came to other exhibits after that as well," says Orffmann. "The exhibition put museum-going on the map as a leisure time interest. It had never been as popular as after that event." And that may be the real treasure of Tutankhamen.

Recording Karnak

A team of scholars from the University of Memphis is documenting and analyzing the carved scenes and inscriptions found in the Great Hypostyle Hall and the temple of the god Amon-Re at Karnak, the site of the largest temple complex in Egypt. The work creates a permanent record of the sculptures, which are slowly deteriorating, and provides insight into Egyptian religious ideology.

Exhibitions on Ancient Egypt

Mummies and Magic: The Funerary Arts of Ancient Egypt
Museum of Fine Arts, Boston

Ancient Nubia: Egypt's Rival in Africa
University o Pfennsylvania

Cleopatra's Egypt: Art and Culture in the Ptolemaic Period
Brooklyn Museum

Amenhotep III and His World
Cleveland Museum of Art

Coptic Egypt: Art and Ideas from the Second to Seventh Centuries
Rhode Island School of Design

The First Egyptians: The Origins of Civilizations in Predynastic Egypt
University of South Carolina, Columbia

Temples, Tombs, and the Egyptian Universe
Brooklyn Museum

Pharaohs of the Sun: Akhenaten, Nefertiti, Tutankhamen
Museum of Fine Arts, Boston

The Carnegie Museum of Natural History, the Brooklyn Museum, and the Walters Art Gallery reinstalled their Egyptian collections, which included the development of new gallery guides, public programs, and educational programs for school children.

Chinese Art Treasures

China's culture is widely regarded as unique in its continuity—the culture of modern China has demonstrable roots in the culture of the China of 5,000 years ago. However, within that long continuity there has been dazzling innovation, rich diversity, and profound transformation, as demonstrated in a wide-ranging exhibition mounted at several Guggenheim Museums in 1998.

"China: 5,000 Years" explored innovation and transformation in Chinese art over a period of five millennia, assembling more than two hundred treasures from seventeen Chinese provinces. The exhibition demonstrated at least two paradoxes in Chinese culture. One is that while the continuity of the culture would suggest a profound conservatism, Chinese art was often daring and innovative. The other has to do with the fact that many Chinese cultural artifacts survived underground, not above ground, and were not unearthed until after the founding of the People's Republic. Although the culture may have been continuous, the knowledge of many of its artifacts is new.

Jade, for example, "the fairest of stones," is widely appreciated in Chinese art, literature, and culture, but it was only after recent excavations that scholars knew there were at least three jade-working cultures in Neolithic times. The exhibition showed wide-ranging examples of the use of jade from 3600 B.C. until the end of the Qing dynasty in A.D.1911. Eight other areas of artistic production were included: ritual bronzes from the Shang and Zhou dynasties, tomb ceramics from the Qin and Han through the Tang periods (221 B.C.–A.D. 907), lacquerware, sculpture, landscape painting, and calligraphy, including rare early Song handscrolls.

The exhibition was four years in preparation and was hailed as a major event in Sino-American cultural exchange. It required an unprecedented collaboration for American museum officials with the Ministry of Culture and the National Administration for Cultural Heritage of the People's Republic of China. The end result was the largest exhibition of such art ever to be seen outside China.

China on Film

Three films explore China's turbulent twentieth century: ***China in Revolution, 1911–1949*** charts the establishment of the Chinese Communist state. ***The Mao Years, 1949–1976*** continues the story from the Communist takeover until the death of Mao Zedong and the end of the Cultural Revolution in 1976. ***The Gate of Heavenly Peace*** considers the 1989 Tiananmen Square protests in the context of Chinese political attitudes and habits.

Chronicling China

The Cambridge History of China, some sixteen volumes, spans Chinese civilization and offers the first modern overview of Chinese history. Contributors to the work include scholars from China, Australia, England, France, Canada, Singapore, and the United States.

Exhibitions on China

Three other major Endowment-supported traveling exhibitions brought Chinese culture to cities across the country:

The Great Bronze Age in China
Sponsored by the Metropolitan Museum of Art, the exhibition featured the first comprehensive collection of Chinese Bronze Age artifacts to be shown in the Western Hemisphere. The exhibition traveled to Chicago, Fort Worth, Los Angeles, and Boston.

Archaeological Treasures from the People's Republic of China
More than one million visitors in San Francisco and Kansas City saw this exhibition of recently excavated objects dating from 600,000 B.C. to the fourteenth century A.D.

Splendors of Imperial China: Treasures from the National Palace Museum, Taipei
The exhibition was seen in New York City, Washington, D.C., and San Francisco. The exhibition featured more than 350 objects drawn from the personal collections of China's emperors. It was organized by the Metropolitan Museum of Art.

Classics Online

The marriage of computer technology and ancient literature is approaching its thirtieth anniversary. Although hardly imaginable three decades ago, it is now taken for granted that a humanities scholar can sit at his or her computer and with a click of the mouse instantly call up almost any ancient Greek text.

Two NEH-supported projects have been at the forefront of putting ancient texts in digital format: the *Thesaurus Linguae Graecae* (TLG) at the University of California at Irvine, and the Perseus Project at Tufts University.

The TLG (www.tlg.uci.edu/) contains virtually all ancient Greek texts surviving from the period between Homer (eighth century B.C.) and A.D. 600, and a large number of texts from the period between A.D. 600 and the fall of Constantinople in 1453. The TLG texts are provided in CD-ROM format and are available in more than fifty countries. The project's fifth and latest CD-ROM contains seventy-six million words of text from seven thousand works by thirty-five hundred authors.

"The TLG was the first electronic project in the humanities," says Maria Pantelia, director of the TLG Project. The computerized data bank was the brainchild of Professor Marianne McDonald, who, as a graduate student in 1972, saw the value of computers in manipulating large amounts of data. Her concept was put in place with the help of David Packard and his team of computer experts. Scholars had tried to catalog surviving Greek literature for the past four centuries; it was only with the advent of computer technology that they succeeded. Pantelia admits that classicists are considered conservative by nature and the irony of ancient texts being distributed through this high-tech means is not lost on her. But the speed and volume of texts available on computer has turned scholars into high-tech converts.

Vergil's Roman World

The University of Pennsylvania is developing *The Vergil Project* (vergil.classics. upenn.edu/), an online, interactive hypertext database of all materials related to the life and writings of Roman epic poet Vergil. The university also hosted two summer seminars for schoolteachers on "Vergil's Aeneid in Its Augustan Context." Scholars at the University of California, Los Angeles, are translating the treatises of Philodemus, a Hellenistic philosopher who was a teacher of Vergil and a transmitter of Greek thought to the Romans.

"Take St. John of Chrysostom, for example," she says. "Its 4.5 million words can be searched in seconds. This is the TLG's main contribution. But also being able to find all extant literature gives scholars access to a huge library with texts many didn't even know existed." The TLG staff continues to add new texts from the Byzantine and post-Byzantine period.

The Perseus Project (www.perseus.tufts.edu) calls itself "an evolving digital library," referring to its continually increasing selection of offerings. The project is named after the hero from Greek mythology, says Editor-in-Chief Gregory Crane, because he wanted a character "who reflected going out into the greater world of gods and monsters."

Containing more than thirty thousand images and five million words of text, Perseus offers a number of innovative tools that change the way students approach ancient languages, literature, and archaeology. Users can read English translations of the plays of Euripides, the poetry of Homer, or the history of Thucydides. Students of Greek and Latin are able to flip back and forth from the original text to the English translation, reinforcing their understanding of the ancient languages. "People can use the texts even if they don't know the languages very well. And the project has vastly increased access to visual information," Crane says. Viewers interested in sculpture, for example, can see large color photos—sometimes twenty or more shots of the same object—taken from different angles.

Originally containing information about ancient Greece, Perseus's topics have expanded to include Rome, ancient science, nineteenth-century City of London, and the complete works of Christopher Marlowe. By the end of 2000, Perseus will house more materials from the English Renaissance, including the complete works of William Shakespeare. Text and images about ancient Egypt and the American Civil War are also in the works.

"Perseus is like a library that belongs to all of us, to students and faculty and to scholars and students who are not affiliated with any university," says Laura Gibbs, assistant professor of classics and letters at the University of Oklahoma. "And it is open twenty-four hours a day."

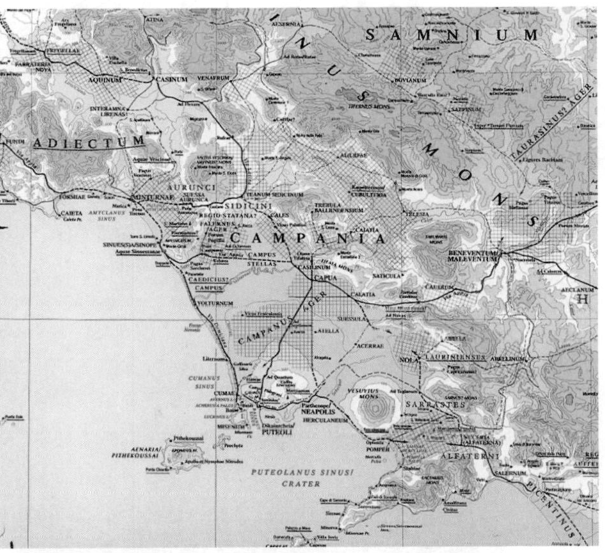

An Atlas Worthy of a Titan

The Barrington Atlas of the Greek and Roman World **offers a comprehensive set of maps from archaic Greece to the Late Roman Empire, providing students and military history buffs with a valuable resource. Under the direction of Richard Talbert, a professor of ancient history at University of North Carolina, Chapel Hill, more than seventy experts used satellite-generated aeronautical charts, archaeological discoveries, and up to date historical scholarship to reconstruct the geography of the ancient world.**

Unearthing Ancient Greece

With NEH support, archaeologists have excavated Halai in East Lokris on the coast north of Athens, providing important clues about life outside Greek urban centers. Excavations have also been conducted at the Sanctuary of Poseidon on the Isthmus of Corinth, revealing new information about the popular festivals held to honor the sea god.

An Imperial Adventure

"Opinions differ about the British Empire; there can be no such disagreement about this superb history of it," observed David Cannadine in the *Times Literary Supplement* in praise of the five-volume *Oxford History of the British Empire* (OHBE). Published in 1998 and 1999, the OHBE tells the story of the rise and fall of the British Empire by emphasizing British interaction with other cultures. Using empire as a window into world history, the OHBE demonstrates how events in Britain combined with those elsewhere to create a territorial empire and constantly changing social and economic relationships.

The OHBE was the brainchild of Wm. Roger Louis, the Kerr Chair in English History and Culture at the University of Texas at Austin and a Fellow of St. Antony's College, Oxford. Asked by Oxford University Press in 1992 to review a proposal for a history of the British Empire that would cover each colony and dependency—eventually reaching some 75 volumes—Louis judged it unworkable.

Talking over the idea with his colleagues, however, he was struck by their enthusiasm for a new history. *The Cambridge History of the British Empire*, begun in 1929 and finished in 1959, read like a period piece, reflecting the era's anxieties over constitutional issues and decolonization. Also working in favor of a new history was the recent cooling of tensions in colonial studies, a field where ideological passions about Afro-Asian nationalism and anti-imperialism fueled long-simmering debates. The cooling made it possible to bring together area experts—historians of India, Africa, Asia, and the Middle East—and historians who usually write about empire from the British vantage point.

At a conference in May 1994, thirty historians sketched a rough outline for what would eventually become the OHBE: a multi-volume work roughly divided by centuries. Louis accepted responsibility for organizing the project and assembled an international team of editors. Nicholas Canny of the National University of Ireland took on the task of describing the origins of empire. Peter Marshall, president of the Royal Historical Society, agreed to edit the eighteenth-century volume, and Andrew Porter, Rhodes Professor of Imperial History at King's College, London, took on the nineteenth-century volume. Judith Brown, Beit Professor at Oxford, teamed with Louis to edit the twentieth-century volume. Yale University's

Robin Winks assumed responsibility for the volume on historiography.

At this point, Louis turned to NEH for support for the project, which had already received funding from the Rhodes Trust. The first proposal did not receive funding. Project reviewers cited the need for more extensive treatment of some of the Asian and African themes and the inclusion of more area specialists. Taking the criticisms to heart, Louis and his editors added chapters and recruited new authors. The OHBE's second application met with success. Using an NEH collaborative research grant, Louis and his editorial team brought together the more than one hundred historians working on the OHBE for a September 1995 conference to discuss their contributions. The grant also covered the cost of circulating draft chapters and funded the appointment of an associate editor, Alaine Low, to manage the project on a day to day basis.

It was only three years from the conference until the publication of the first volume—a short period for completing a project of this scope and size. The process was hastened along by Louis's insistence that authors who did not meet their deadlines would be removed from the project. While the policy meant the loss of a few historians, it ensured that the research behind the OHBE would be fresh. The pairing of cutting-edge scholarship and deft writing makes the OHBE prime reading for both academics and the general public. But it also provides something else: a starting point for the next generation to begin asking questions about empire and cross-cultural relations.

Along the Silk Road

A CD-ROM from the Asia Society of New York uses role-playing to explore the process of cultural exchange in history. Students can follow a sixteenth-century Jesuit priest, an eighth-century princess, or a nineteenth-century archaeologist along the Silk Road, the ancient trade route that once spanned 5,000 miles from Turkey to China.

The Glory of Byzantium

Through an exhibition and public programs, the Metropolitan Museum of Art examined the art and culture of the second golden age of Byzantium (843–1261) and the influence of the Byzantine Empire beyond its borders.

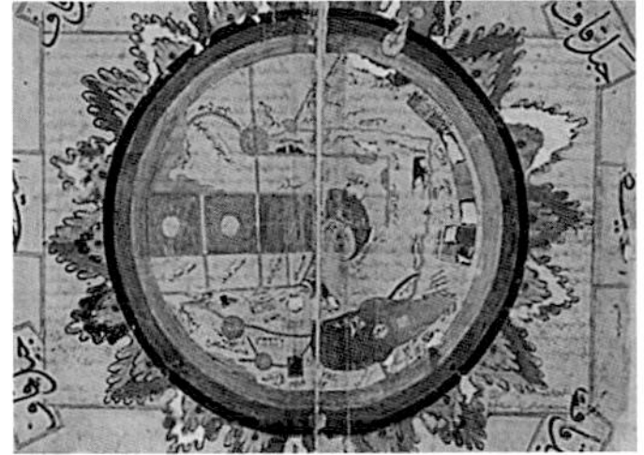

Mapping the World

The six-volume *History of Cartography* looks at maps in the context of the societies that made and used them. Organized by region and time period, the volumes integrate existing scholarship with new research, examining an unprecedented range of artifacts from local maps to those of the cosmos.

The Colonial Experience

North Carolina's National Humanities Center hosted two summer institutes for schoolteachers that considered how the history of colonialism in Latin America, India, and Africa can be used to teach non-Western history.

My History Is America's History

Your great-grandmother's footprints might be on the Oregon Trail. Members of your family might have fought in the Civil War or struggled for equality in the Civil Rights movement. Everything you have discovered about your ancestors' lives—names, dates, and movements from place to place—fits into the larger story of the nation's past.

Follow your family's history and you will discover America's history. That is the theme of My History Is America's History, a project created by NEH to mark the millennium. The search can begin with an old photograph, a letter, a name on a military roster.

Julia Fong wanted to trace her grandfather, who came from China to California with falsified documents—a "paper son" to a merchant in Sacramento. He died when she was a year old. She interviewed relatives, visited the Angel Island Immigration Center, examined immigration files, and even traveled to China to trace her grandfather's journey.

In French Island, Maine, residents documented the history of the town's disappearing French-speaking community. They gathered oral histories and created a photographic archive, an illustrated history of the community, and a website.

According to James Horton, adviser to the My History project and the Benjamin Banneker Professor of American Studies and History at George Washington University, "We're all important in the nation's history, but people tend to make a distinction between their history and America's history. This new project is about connecting yourself to the nation's history." In his own work, Horton used records from the National Archives to trace the life of a nineteenth-century slave in Washington, D.C., named Edward Ambush. Horton

Preserving Artifacts

Museums and archives across the country have used NEH grants to improve the storage and environmental conditions of more than twenty-eight million objects, allowing them to be passed on to future generations.

SEGUNDA EDICION

LA PRENSA

NUEVA YORK, SABADO 14 DE FEBRERO DE 1931.

VOL. XXVI.—NUMERO 4085.

Inicia campaña de economía el gobierno chileno

BECADOS CHILENOS EN ESTADOS UNIDOS

Galicia recibe a tiros al primer candidato de los primorriveristas

Hay perspectiva de paz en la historia de la India inglesa

La juez Jean Norris confiesa haber alterado un expediente del juzgado

Ecuador busca un plan de economías en su presupuesto

NICARAGUA SERA ABA POR LOS "MARINES

El secretario de E que en junio no

V STOPÁCH ČASU . . .

When Disaster Strikes

NEH teamed up with the Federal Emergency Management Agency, the Getty Conservation Institute, and the National Institute for the Conservation of Cultural Property to help protect the nation's cultural heritage from the ravages of natural disasters by creating the Emergency Response and Salvage Wheel. The wheel provides staff at cultural institutions with quick access to essential information on how to salvage collections. The steps taken in the first forty-eight hours after disaster strikes are crucial to limiting the extent of the damage. More than 45,000 libraries, museums, archives, and historical organizations and sites nationwide have received the wheel.

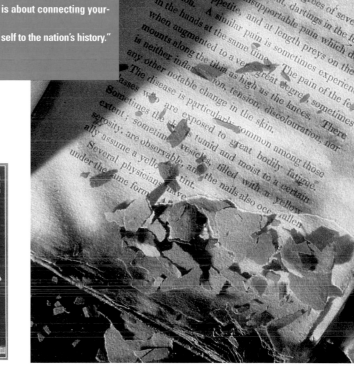

"We're all important in the nation's history, but people tend to make a distinction between their history and America's history. This new project is about connecting yourself to the nation's history."

examined freedom papers, personal correspondence, the city directory, and the 1850 census. "From these documents I learned about slavery, the life of a person going from slavery to freedom, and other information about the community," says Horton. "These kinds of documents can be used to trace a family or a broader community."

The "front porch" of the My History Is America's History project is a website—www.myhistory.org—where visitors post their family stories They also link up with news articles, maps, photographs, and timelines that can help them in their research. Teachers use the website to bring the project into the classroom, allowing them to use family stories to make history real for their students. Information is also available about history workshops, exhibitions, and programs all over the country.

NEH Chairman William Ferris says, "We hope that this project will bring together all the different kinds of work on family history already being done. If that happens, the human element of our country's history will be richer for it."

Saving Brittle Books

Eighty million volumes in the nation's research libraries are disintegrating because of the fragility of their paper. In 1989, NEH launched a nationally coordinated program to preserve the intellectual content of approximately three million brittle books through preservation microfilming. More than 860,000 endangered volumes have been microfilmed to date.

YORKSKÝ DENNÍK

(CZECHOSLOVAK DAILY PUBLISHED IN SLOVAK LANGUAGE)

NEW YORK, PIATOK, dňa 31. marca. FRIDAY, March 31, 1933.

ŽIDIA ŽIADAJÚ HINDENBURGA, ABY PREKAZIL BOJKOTOVANIE

LEHMAN ŽIADA "SLUŠNÝ" DOZOR PREDAJU PIVA.

ČO NOVÉHO V KRAJI...

PRESIDENT NEMECKA VŠAK SOTVA VOLAČO PODNIKNE.

Francia uvažuje o pláne Mussoliniho.

Extra! Extra!

The United States Newspaper Program is rescuing a piece of history by cataloging and microfilming fifty-seven million pages from 133,000 newspapers dating from the early days of the Republic.

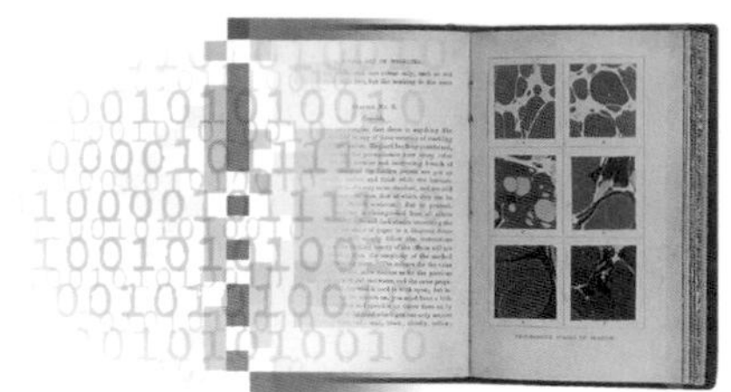

A Technological Revolution

When NEH was created in 1965, the idea of merging computers and the humanities seemed fanciful. A computer could make sophisticated calculations for a trip to the moon, but what did it have to offer humanities scholars? As it turns out—plenty.

Scholars have harnessed the computer not only to change how research is done, but also to take cultural learning digital. Classrooms and living rooms across the country now have access to online dictionaries, encyclopedias, electronic archives, and digital libraries.

The first revolutionary wave came in the use of databases to organize large quantities of information. *The English Short Title Catalog*, which details all books published in English from 1473 to 1801, transformed the study of British and colonial history. Doing a keyword search, a scholar in Iowa can identify pamphlets printed to denounce the Boston Tea Party or comment on Dryden's poetry—even if the only copy is held by a library in New Zealand. Another database is set to transform African American history. The recently completed *Trans-Atlantic Slave Trade Database* will help historians chart the origin and eventual home of slaves brought from Africa to America from 1650 to 1867.

The next digital wave came with the advent of the World Wide Web in the nineties. Originally developed as a way for a small group of scientists to share data, in a little over a decade, the Web has dramatically changed the way information is communicated. Humanists have taken advantage of the Web's multimedia environment to increase access to primary sources.

The Web's ability to display images has been a real boon for the study of ancient cultures. One key source of information about daily life in ancient Egypt and Greece is texts written on papyrus. Scholars have not made extensive use of papyrus because of its fragility—manuscripts are frequently more than 3,000 years old—and fragments of one document can be held by two or three institutions. To make the manuscripts easier to use and preserve their content, Columbia University has launched the Papyri Project, which is digitizing the papyrus collections held by six libraries in the United States, plus one in France. When complete, scholars will be able to view images of and study 30,000 documents online, ranging from tax records to legal files to literary works. A similar project for cuneiform manuscripts is being masterminded by UCLA.

The William Blake Archive (http://jefferson.village.virginia.edu/blake/) at the University of Virginia is pairing up poetry and paintings. When Blake's poems were first published in the late eighteenth and early nineteenth centuries, they were accompanied by paintings done in his own hand. Over the next two hundred years, Blake's poems were reprinted, but without the art, making finding a complete manuscript no easy task. The archive has digitized sixteen of Blake's nineteen illuminated works, allowing users to view the poetry and artwork as they were originally meant to be seen. This digital rendition of Blake's work offers exciting new possibilities for literary scholars and art historians, who have traditionally studied them separately.

Other projects are giving the spoken word a more central place. Michigan State University's *The National Gallery of the Spoken Word* (www.ngsw.org) is digitizing more than 50,000 speeches, performances, lectures, interviews, and broadcasts by people from all walks of life. The recordings will be searchable by keyword. Included are Thomas Edison's first cylinder recordings, the voices of Babe Ruth and Florence Nightingale, and Studs Terkel's interviews. Northwestern University's *Oyez, Oyez, Oyez* (http://oyez.nwu.edu), a website about the history of the Supreme Court, features recordings of oral arguments. Limited to only fifteen minutes to sway the justices of the merits of their case, lawyers before the court offer finely tuned arguments.

The Internet has also created e-communities that bring scholars together to talk about the humanities. Hosted by Michigan State University, H-Net sponsors more than one hundred interactive newsletters. The listservs, which are edited by scholars, reach more than 90,000 subscribers in ninety countries. By logging into their e-mail accounts, H-Net subscribers learn about conferences, new books, archival access, and grant opportunities, and exchange advice about effective classroom teaching.

All of these projects are driven by vast amounts of data that, without careful planning, can become damaged or incompatible with new technologies. To help solve storage and migration problems, NEH has supported the development of guidelines and methods for the production and preservation of digital materials. One such project, the Text Encoding Initiative (TEI), produced a set of guidelines used by more than sixty electronic text centers, digital libraries, and Web-based projects in North America and Europe.

Looking toward the future of humanities computing, NEH joined a number of other federal agencies in 1998 to sponsor the Digital Library Initiative. Grants given under the program devise creative solutions to digitizing difficult materials and develop new approaches to preserving digital documents. When the projects are complete, users will be able to determine the meaning of an ancient Chinese word, compare various renditions of classical music scores while reading the sheet music, and explore an ancient Egyptian tomb.

NEH's contribution to the digital revolution can be summed up in one word: content. By supporting projects that bring texts, paintings, sculpture, music, speeches, and critical commentary into the online world, NEH has changed how Americans learn about the humanities. Cultural learning is no longer limited by geography—now it's just a matter of point and click.

EDSITEment

The vast array of resources available on the Internet poses challenges for parents and teachers seeking high-quality humanities material. Using EDSITEment (http://edsitement.neh.gov) takes the guesswork out of whether a website's content is reliable. Websites included on EDSITEment have been screened using a rigorous merit review process, endorsed by a panel of educators, and deemed appropriate for classroom use. To be included, websites must have strong educational content and superior design.

Users can browse EDSITEment websites by topic—literature, foreign language, art and culture, and history—or do keyword searches. EDSITEment also features lesson plans for teachers to use or adapt to their own needs.

EDSITEment is the product of a partnership forged in the spring of 1997 between NEH, the Council of Great City Schools, MCI WorldCom Foundation, and the National Trust for the Humanities. In the fall of 2000, it included 105 websites.

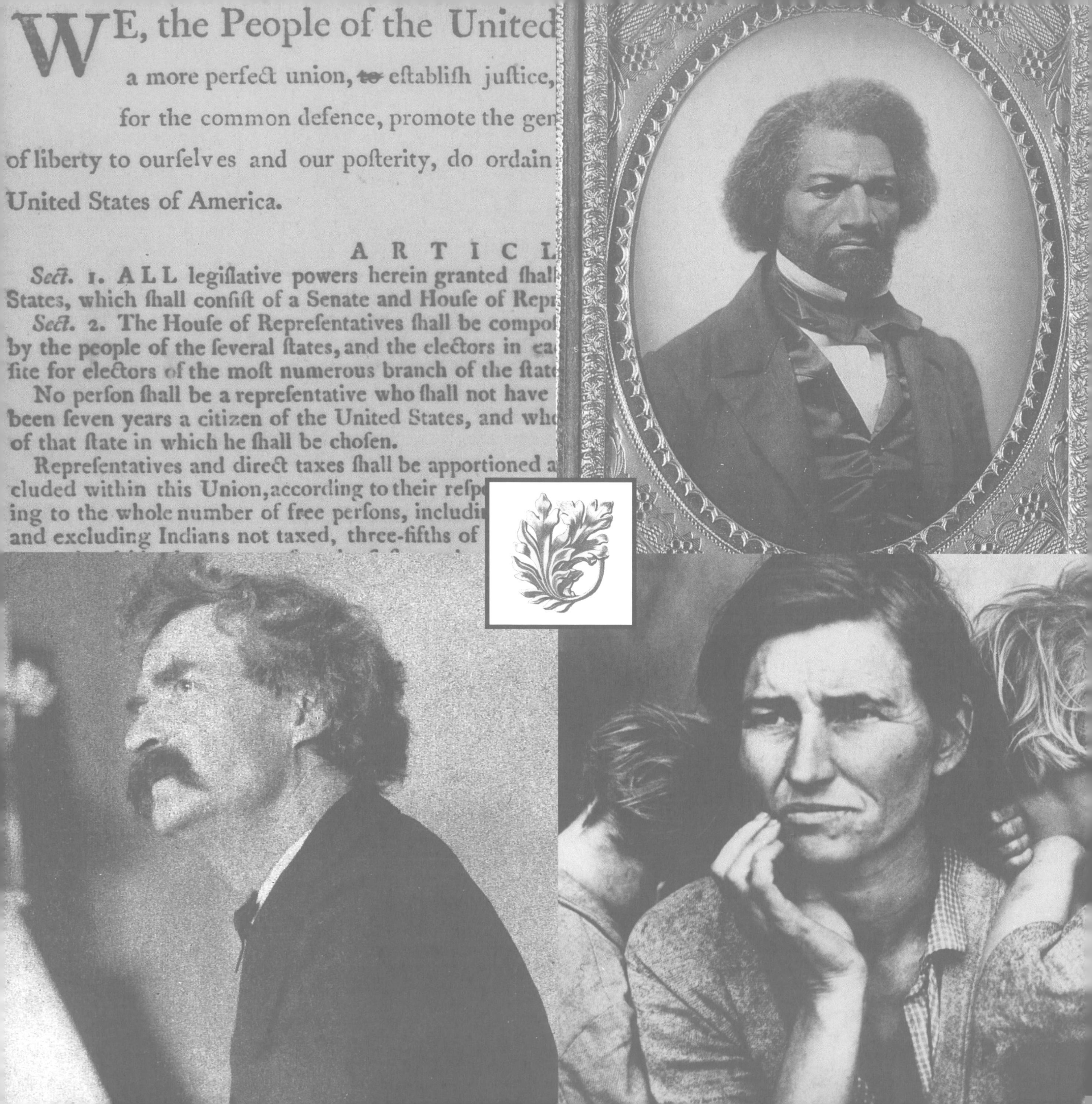
WE, the People of the United
a more perfect union, to establish justice,
for the common defence, promote the
of liberty to ourselves and our posterity, do ordain
United States of America.
ARTIC
Sect. 1. ALL legislative powers herein granted shall
States, which shall consist of a Senate and House of
Sect. 2. The House of Representatives shall be
by the people of the several states, and the electors in
site for electors of the most numerous branch of the
No person shall be a representative who shall not have
been seven years a citizen of the United States, and
of that state in which he shall be chosen.
Representatives and direct taxes shall be apportioned
cluded within this Union, according to their
ing to the whole number of free persons,
and excluding Indians not taxed, three-fifths of

Prizes and People

Pulitzer Prize

Bancroft Prize

Jefferson Lecture in the Humanities

Charles Frankel Prize

National Humanities Medal

Chairmen of NEH

National Council on the Humanities

Pulitzer Prize

Books written and published with NEH support have received fourteen Pulitzer Prizes. The Pulitzer Prize has been awarded annually since 1917. Administered by Columbia University, the prize recognizes works of exceptional merit in all areas of journalism, fiction, nonfiction, history, biography, and poetry.

1975 Pulitzer Prize for Letters in History
DUMAS MALONE
Jefferson and His Time
(Boston: Little, Brown, 1968–75)

1976 Pulitzer Prize in Journalism
JAMES RISSER
Des Moines Register

1979 Pulitzer Prize in History
DON E. FEHRENBACHER
The Dred Scott Case: Its Significance in American Law and Politics
(New York: Oxford University Press, 1978)

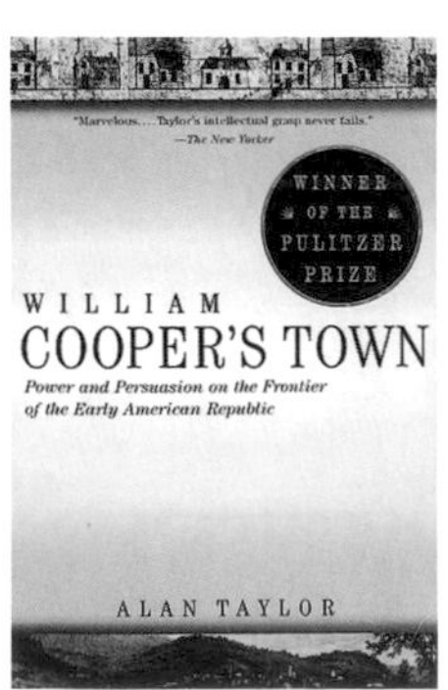

1979 Pulitzer Prize in Journalism
JAMES RISSER
Des Moines Register

1986 Pulitzer Prize in Biography
ELIZABETH FRANK
Louise Bogan: A Portrait
(New York: Alfred A. Knopf, 1985)

1987 Pulitzer Prize for Letters in History
BERNARD BAILYN
Voyagers to the West: A Passage in the Peopling of America on the Eve of the Revolution
(New York: Alfred A. Knopf, 1986)

1988 Pulitzer Prize in History
JAMES M. MCPHERSON
Battle Cry of Freedom: The Civil War Era
(New York: Oxford University Press, 1988)

1990 Pulitzer Prize in History
LAUREL T. ULRICH
A Midwife's Tale: The Life of Martha Ballard, Based on Her Diary, 1785–1812
(New York: Alfred A. Knopf, 1990)

1994 Pulitzer Prize in Biography
JOAN D. HEDRICK
Harriet Beecher Stowe: A Life
(New York: Oxford University Press, 1994)

1996 Pulitzer Prize in History
ALAN TAYLOR
William Cooper's Town: Power and Persuasion on the Frontier of the Early American Republic
(New York: Alfred A. Knopf, 1995)

1997 Pulitzer Prize in History
JACK RAKOVE
Original Meanings: Politics and Ideas in the Making of the Constitution
(New York: Alfred A. Knopf, 1997)

1999 Pulitzer Prize in History
EDWIN G. BURROWS AND MIKE WALLACE
Gotham: A History of New York City to 1898
(New York: Oxford University Press, 1998)

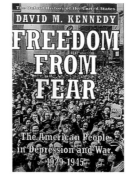

2000 Pulitzer Prize for History
DAVID M. KENNEDY
Freedom from Fear: The American People in Depression and War, 1929–1945
(New York: Oxford University Press, 1999)

2000 Pulitzer Prize for Biography
STACY SCHIFF
Vera (Mrs. Vladimir Nabokov)
(New York: Random House, 1999)

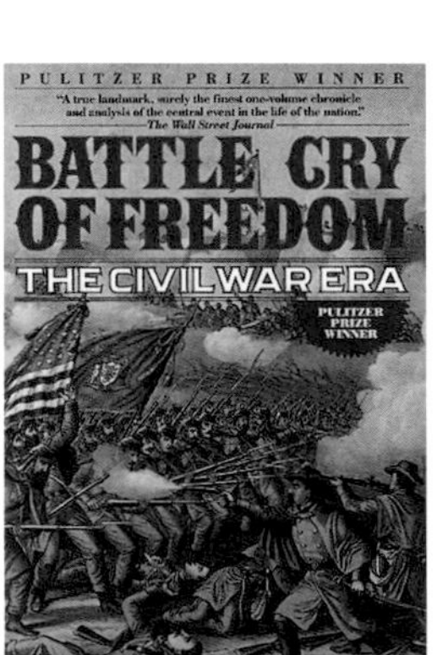

Bancroft Prize

Books written and published with NEH support have received seventeen Bancroft Prizes. The Bancroft Prize has been awarded annually by Columbia University since 1948. The prize recognizes books of exceptional merit in American history, biography, or diplomacy.

1970 Bancroft Prize
GORDON S. WOOD
The Creation of the American Republic, 1776–1787
(Chapel Hill: The University of North Carolina Press, 1969)

1976 Bancroft Prize
R.W. B. LEWIS
Edith Wharton: A Biography
(New York: Harper and Row, 1975)

1980 Bancroft Prize (co-winner)
ROBERT DALLEK
Franklin D. Roosevelt and American Foreign Policy, 1932–1945 (New York: Oxford University Press, 1979)

1980 Bancroft Prize (co-winner)
THOMAS DUBLIN
Women at Work: The Transformation of Work and Community in Lowell, Massachusetts, 1826–1860
(New York: Columbia University Press, 1979)

1981 Bancroft Prize (co-winner)
EDWARD COUNTRYMAN
A People in Revolution: The American Revolution and Political Society in New York, 1760–1790
(Baltimore: The Johns Hopkins University Press, 1981)

1981 Bancroft Prize (co-winner)
JEAN STROUSE
Alice James: A Biography
(Boston: Houghton Mifflin Company, 1980)

1983 Bancroft Prize
NICHOLAS A. SALVATORE
Eugene V. Debs: Citizen and Socialist
(Urbana: University of Illinois Press, 1983)

1988 Bancroft Prize
ERIC FONER
Reconstruction: America's Unfinished Revolution, 1863–1877
(New York: Harper and Row, 1988)

1990 Bancroft Prize (co-winner)
NEIL R. MCMILLEN
Dark Journey: Black Missisippians in the Age of Jim Crow
(Champaign: University of Illinois Press, 1989)

1990 Bancroft Prize (co-winner)
LAUREL T. ULRICH
A Midwife's Tale: The Life of Martha Ballard, Based on Her Diary, 1785–1812
(New York: Alfred A. Knopf, 1990)

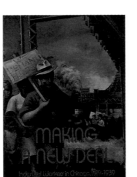

1991 Bancroft Prize
LIZABETH COHEN
Making a New Deal: Industrial Workers in Chicago, 1919–1939
(New York: Cambridge University Press, 1990)

1993 Bancroft Prize
MELVYN P. LEFFLER
A Preponderance of Power: National Security, the Truman Administration, and the Cold War
(Stanford: Stanford University Press, 1992)

1994 Bancroft Prize
WINTHROP JORDAN
Tumult and Silence at Second Creek: An Inquiry Into a Civil War Slave Conspiracy
(Baton Rouge: Louisiana State University Press, 1993)

1996 Bancroft Prize (co-winner)
DAVID S. REYNOLDS
Walt Whitman's America: A Cultural Biography
(New York: Alfred A. Knopf, 1995)

1996 Bancroft Prize (co-winner)
ALAN TAYLOR
William Cooper's Town: Power and Persuasion on the Frontier of the Early American Republic
(New York: Alfred A. Knopf, 1995)

1997 Bancroft Prize
DAVID E. KYVIG
Explicit and Authentic Acts: Amending the U.S. Constitution, 1776–1995 (Lawrence: University of Kansas Press, 1996)

2000 Bancroft Prize
JAMES H. MERRELL
Into the American Woods: Negotiators on the Pennsylvania Frontier
(New York: W.W. Norton, 2000)

Jefferson Lecture in the Humanities

NEH established the annual Jefferson Lecture in the Humanities in 1972. Selection as Jefferson Lecturer is the highest honor the federal government confers for distinguished achievement in the humanities. Created to honor the intellectual and civic virtues exemplified by Thomas Jefferson, the lectureship recognizes supreme scholarship in the humanities and provides an occasion to communicate the knowledge and wisdom of the humanities to a broad general audience. The Jefferson Lecture is held each spring in Washington, D.C. The lecturer receives an honorarium of $10,000.

The Jefferson Lecturer is selected by the National Council on the Humanities. Nominations are solicited from scholarly societies, cultural and historical organizations, public and private institutions, and other interested parties located throughout the United States. A special committee of NEH Council members considers the nominees, ultimately recommending a list of finalists for consideration by the full Council.

1972
LIONEL TRILLING
Mind in the Modern World

1973
ERIK ERIKSON
Dimensions of a New Identity

1974
ROBERT PENN WARREN
Poetry and Democracy

1975
PAUL A. FREUND
Liberty: The Great Disorder of Speech

1976
JOHN HOPE FRANKLIN
Racial Equality in America

1977
SAUL BELLOW
The Writer and His Country Look Each Other Over

1978
C. VANN WOODWARD
The European Vision of America

1979
EDWARD SHILS
Render Unto Caesar: Government, Society, and Universities in Their Reciprocal Rights and Duties

1980
BARBARA TUCHMAN
Mankind's Better Moments

1981
GERALD HOLTON
Where Is Science Taking Us?

1982
EMILY T. VERMEULE
Greeks and Barbarians: The Classical Experience in the Larger World

1983
JAROSLAV PELIKAN
The Vindication of Tradition

1984
SIDNEY HOOK
Education in Defense of a Free Society

1985
CLEANTH BROOKS
Literature and Technology

1986
LESZEK KOLAKOWSKI
The Idolatry of Politics

1987
FORREST MCDONALD
The Intellectual World of the Founding Fathers

1988
ROBERT NISBET
The Present Age

1989
WALKER PERCY
The Fateful Rift: The San Andreas Fault in the Modern Mind

1990
BERNARD LEWIS
Western Civilization: A View from the East

1991
GERTRUDE HIMMELFARB
Of Heroes, Villains and Valets

1992
BERNARD M.W. KNOX
The Oldest Dead White European Males

1993
ROBERT CONQUEST
History, Humanity, and Truth

1994
GWENDOLYN BROOKS
Family Pictures

1995
VINCENT SCULLY
The Architecture of Community

1996
TONI MORRISON
The Future of Time: Literature and Diminished Expectations

1997
STEPHEN TOULMIN
A Dissenter's Story

1998
BERNARD BAILYN
To Begin the World Anew: Politics and the Creative Imagination

1999
CAROLINE WALKER BYNUM
Shape and Story: Metamorphosis in the Western Tradition

2000
JAMES M. MCPHERSON
"For a Vast Future Also": Lincoln and the Millennium

Charles Frankel Prize

In 1988, NEH established the Charles Frankel Prize to recognize persons for outstanding contributions to the public's understanding of the humanities. The Charles Frankel Prize was awarded from 1989 through 1996.

1989

PATRICIA L. BATES, reading program specialist who developed a model for scholar-led reading-and-discussion groups now used in libraries across the United States.

DANIEL J. BOORSTIN, Librarian of Congress Emeritus and author of several books on American history and culture for a general audience.

WILLARD L. BOYD, president of Chicago's Field Museum of Natural History and a leader in developing innovative museum programs for the public.

CLAY S. JENKINSON, a leader in the revival of chautauqua, a forum for public discussion about the ideas and lives of key figures in American history.

AMÉRICO PAREDES, author and creator of numerous public programs on folklore and Mexican American culture.

1990

MORTIMER J. ADLER, director of the Institute for Philosophical Research in Chicago and author of numerous works on education and philosophy.

HARRY HAMPTON, independent filmmaker and creator of PBS's *Eyes on the Prize* documentary series.

BERNARD M.W. KNOX, director emeritus of Harvard's Center for Hellenic Studies and author of several books on classical culture for the general reader.

DAVID VAN TASSEL, historian and founder of National History Day, an annual national competition recognizing high school students for excellence in historical research and analysis.

ETHYLE R. WOLFE, architect of Brooklyn College's innovative core curriculum and spokeswoman for liberal arts education.

1991

WINTON BLOUNT, major benefactor of the humanities in Alabama, including the Alabama Shakespeare Festival.

KEN BURNS, independent filmmaker and creator of *The Civil War* documentary series for PBS.

LOUISE COWAN, co-founder of the Dallas Institute of Humanities and Culture, where she created and leads summer academies on literature for teachers and principals.

KARL HAAS, host of radio's *Adventures in Good Music* program.

JOHN TCHEN, historian and co-founder of New York's Chinatown History Museum.

1992

ALLAN BLOOM, philosopher, educator, and author of the best-selling *The Closing of the American Mind*, an influential critique of American higher education.

SHELBY FOOTE, novelist, historian, and principal commentator in the PBS documentary *The Civil War*.

RICHARD RODRIGUEZ, writer-journalist and author of *Hunger of Memory*, a widely read book about American cultural diversity.

HAROLD K. SKRAMSTAD, JR., president of the Henry Ford Museum & Greenfield Village in Dearborn, Michigan, and innovator in presenting history in museums.

EUDORA WELTY, Pulitzer Prize-winning author whose work has illuminated life in America.

1993

RICARDO E. ALEGRÍA, historian of Caribbean culture and leader in public humanities programming in his native Puerto Rico.

JOHN HOPE FRANKLIN, historian of the American South, educator and pioneering scholar of African American studies.

HANNA HOLBORN GRAY, University of Chicago president emerita and longtime spokesperson for excellence in liberal arts curricula in higher education.

ANDREW HEISKELL, founding chairman of the President's Commission on the Arts and Humanities and longtime benefactor of the humanities.

LAUREL T. ULRICH, pioneering historian of women in New England's past and Pulitzer Prize-winning author.

1994

ERNEST L. BOYER, president of the Carnegie Foundation for the Advancement of Teaching and a national leader in educational reform at all levels.

WILLIAM KITTREDGE, writer and educator whose work has contributed to the development of regional studies of the American West.

PEGGY WHITMAN PRENSHAW, Southern literature scholar and leader in public humanities programming in Mississippi and Louisiana.

Sharon Percy Rockefeller, public broadcasting leader dedicated to reaching wider audiences through quality programming in the arts and humanities.

Dorothy Porter Wesley, librarian whose pioneering work as an archivist of African Americana helped lay the foundation of African American studies programs.

1995

William R. Ferris, director of the Center for the Study of Southern Culture and a prominent scholar of the American South.

Charles Kuralt, author and longtime correspondent at CBS News who chronicled contemporary American life for many years through his "On the Road" pieces.

David Macaulay, author and illustrator of many prize-winning books that rank him among the nation's foremost popularizers of great ideas in architectural history.

David McCullough, Pulitzer Prize-winning author, public television host, champion of historic preservation, and one of the nation's best-known public historians.

Bernice Johnson Reagon, singer-composer, performer, museum curator, and historian dedicated to recovering, preserving, and interpreting African American vocal music.

1996

Rita Dove, Pulitzer Prize-winning poet, former poet laureate of the United States, and an activist in poetry programs for the public.

Doris Kearns Goodwin, Pulitzer Prize-winning historian and a leading scholar of the American presidency, known for her commentary in television news programs and historical documentaries.

Daniel Kemmis, political philosopher, author, civic activist, and director of the Center for the Rocky Mountain West.

Arturo Madrid, professor of Latino literature who, as founding president of the Tomás Rivera Center, helped develop the field of Latino studies in the United States.

Bill Moyers, television journalist who is nationally known for his documentary explorations of ideas and issues in contemporary American life.

National Humanities Medal

The National Humanities Medal, inaugurated in 1997, honors individuals or groups whose work has deepened the nation's understanding of the humanities, broadened our engagement with the humanities, or helped preserve and expand access to important resources in the humanities. Up to twelve medals can be awarded each year.

1997

Nina M. Archabal, director of the Minnesota Historical Society and leader in developing innovative museum programs for the public.

David A. Berry, executive director of the Community College Humanities Association and leading national advocate for improved humanities education in two-year colleges.

Richard J. Franke, businessman and former investment firm CEO, creator of the annual Chicago Humanities Festival, longtime leader of national and state cultural commissions promoting the arts and humanities.

William Friday, executive director of the William Rand Kenan, Jr., Charitable Trust, former university president, leader in promoting excellence in humanities education.

Don Henley, member of The Eagles rock group; founder and chairman of the Walden Woods Project for the preservation of historically significant land; major funder for the Thoreau Institute, the nation's premier center for Thoreau studies.

Maxine Hong Kingston, teacher and writer whose novels about the Chinese American experience have won numerous awards.

Luis Leal, literary scholar whose life's work is a major contribution to cultural understanding of Latin America and Hispanic communities in the United States.

Martin E. Marty, renowned scholar of American religious history and director of the University of Chicago's Public Religion Project.

Paul Mellon, philanthropist who has contributed millions of dollars in support of the humanities and the arts; founder of the Andrew W. Mellon Foundation, the nation's largest nonfederal funder of humanities projects.

Studs Terkel, longtime radio talk-show host, Pulitzer Prize-winning author, oral historian whose published interviews chronicle twentieth-century life in the words of hundreds of ordinary Americans.

1998

STEPHEN E. AMBROSE, biographer of Eisenhower and Nixon; author of *Undaunted Courage*, *Citizen Soldiers*, and *D-Day*, three historical books simultaneously on the *New York Times* bestseller list; principal commentator in the PBS documentary films *Lewis and Clark* and *Eisenhower*; chief historical advisor on the film *Saving Private Ryan*.

E. L. DOCTOROW, author of many popular and critically acclaimed novels about America's last one hundred years, including *Ragtime* and *Billy Bathgate*; many of his novels have been adapted to film, and a musical version of *Ragtime* is currently running on Broadway.

DIANA L. ECK, creator and director of the Harvard University-based Pluralism Project, which documents and analyzes America's religious diversity and produced an acclaimed CD-ROM that is now in wide use as a resource for studying the role of religion in American culture.

NANCYE BROWN GAJ, founder and president of MOTHEREAD, Inc., a national family literacy program that enables newly literate adults to improve their reading skills while helping them encourage and guide the learning of their preschool-age children.

HENRY LOUIS GATES, JR., director of Harvard's W. E. B. Du Bois Institute for Afro-American Research; author of the best-selling *Loose Canons: Notes on the Culture Wars* and *Colored People: A Memoir*; coeditor of the *Norton Anthology of African American Literature*.

VARTAN GREGORIAN, educator, administrator and philanthropist; former president of Brown University and of the New York Public Library; current president of the Carnegie Corporation of New York.

RAMÓN EDUARDO RUIZ, scholar and professor of the history of Hispanic America; author of twelve books, including in-depth studies of the Cuban and Mexican revolutions.

ARTHUR M. SCHLESINGER, JR., prolific scholar and professor of American history; two-time Pulitzer Prize winner for *The Age of Jackson* and *A Thousand Days: John F. Kennedy in the White House*; author of *The Disuniting of America*.

GARRY WILLS, syndicated columnist, essayist, and cultural critic; Pulitzer Prize-winner for *Lincoln at Gettysburg*; author of numerous acclaimed books on American culture and history.

1999

PATRICIA M. BATTIN, librarian who organized and led a national campaign to save millions of disintegrating books published between 1850 and 1950; galvanized congressional support for a national program to microfilm these brittle books, thereby preserving their content as a significant part of the record of American civilization.

TAYLOR BRANCH, Pulitzer Prize-winning writer and journalist whose books have earned him the reputation as a national authority on Martin Luther King, Jr., and the Civil Rights movement.

JACQUELYN DOWD HALL, one of the nation's preeminent scholars of the New South; founder and director of the Southern Oral History Project at the University of North Carolina-Chapel Hill, which is shaping scholarship, education, and public programs about the contemporary South.

GARRISON KEILLOR, creator, writer, and host of Minnesota Public Radio's weekly variety program, *A Prairie Home Companion*; host of *The Writer's Almanac*, a five-minute radio program about literature broadcast daily on stations throughout the nation; author of several bestselling books.

JIM LEHRER, journalist; editor and anchor of *The NewsHour with Jim Lehrer*, public television's award-winning nightly news program; author of novels, plays, and memoirs.

JOHN RAWLS, one of the twentieth century's most influential political philosophers, widely read among political scientists, economists, and legal theorists for his views on justice, basic rights, and equal opportunity; author of *A Theory of Justice* and *Political Liberalism*.

STEVEN SPIELBERG, acclaimed filmmaker who has brought history and literature to life for millions of Americans; producer and/or director of Academy Award-winning films *Saving Private Ryan*, *Amistad*, and *Schindler's List*.

AUGUST WILSON, two-time Pulitzer Prize-winning playwright for *The Piano* and *Fences*, whose plays present an epic story of the black experience in America over the course of a century; influential promoter of the advancement and preservation of black theater and performing arts.

Chairmen of NEH

The National Endowment for the Humanities is headed by a chairman who is appointed for a four-year term by the U.S. president with the advice and consent of the Senate. Since the creation of NEH in 1965, seven chairmen have directed the agency.

July 1966 to June 1970
BARNABY C. KEENEY
Nominated by Lyndon Johnson

December 1971 to January 1977
RONALD S. BERMAN
Nominated by Richard Nixon

October 1977 to December 1981
JOSEPH D. DUFFEY
Nominated by Jimmy Carter

December 1981 to February 1985
WILLIAM J. BENNETT
Nominated by Ronald Reagan

May 1986 to January 1993
LYNNE V. CHENEY
Nominated by Ronald Reagan

August 1993 to August 1997
SHELDON HACKNEY
Nominated by William J. Clinton

November 1997 to present
WILLIAM R. FERRIS
Nominated by William J. Clinton

National Council on the Humanities

The National Council on the Humanities advises the Endowment on its work, including reviewing grant applications and making policy recommendations. The twenty-six members of the council, who serve six-year terms, are nominated by the president of the United States and confirmed by the U.S. Senate.

LINDA L. AAKER
November 1999 to present

CAROLINE L. AHMANSON
June 1974 to January 1980

WILLIAM B. ALLEN
July 1984 to April 1987

ROBERT O. ANDERSON
March 1970 to January 1976

GUSTAVE O. ARLT
March 1966 to January 1968

TED ASHLEY
July 1975 to December 1978

JACOB AVSHALOMOV
February 1968 to March 1974

EDWARD L. AYERS
November 1999 to present

ARAM BAKSHIAN, JR.
October 1987 to July 1992

EDMUND F. BALL
March 1966 to January 1972

MICHAEL T. BASS
September 1990 to July 1994

LEWIS W. BECK
February 1970 to July 1974

BRUCE BENSON
September 1990 to May 1997

IRA BERLIN
November 1999 to present

WALTER BERNS
July 1982 to June 1988

ALVIN BERNSTEIN
June 1988 to July 1992

LOUISE A. BLACKWELL
November 1971 to January 1976

ARTHUR I. BLAUSTEIN
May 1997 to present

ANTHONY A. BLISS
April 1965 to September 1968

ROBERT T. BOWER
March 1966 to January 1972

GERMAINE BREÉ
March 1966 to January 1970

PATRICK H. BUTLER
June 1988 to July 1994

PAUL A. CANTOR
July 1992 to November 1999

GEORGE CAREY
July 1982 to June 1988

PEDRO G. CASTILLO
November 1999 to present

LAWRENCE A. CHICKERING
July 1982 to September 1988

KENNETH B. CLARK
March 1966 to January 1972

MARCUS COHN
September 1980 to July 1986

BRUCE COLE
July 1992 to November 1999

SAMUEL DUBOIS COOK
September 1980 to February 1988

HELEN GRAY CRAWFORD
September 1990 to May 1997

MARY J.C. CRESIMORE
July 1984 to January 1992

JOHN D'ARMS
July 1994 to September 1997

NANCY J. DAVIES
July 1975 to January 1982

CONCHA ORTIZ Y PINO DEKLEVEN
July 1976 to January 1982

EDWIN J. DELATTRE
June 1988 to July 1994

ROLAND P. DILLE
September 1980 to October 1986

MARGARET PACE DUCKETT
September 1990 to present

EVELYN EDSON
November 1999 to present

JOHN M. EHLE, JR.
March 1966 to January 1970

GERALD F. ELSE
March 1966 to January 1972

LUIS A. FERRE
June 1974 to August 1977

DAVID FINN
June 1996 to present

LESLIE H. FISHEL
March 1970 to January 1976

HILLEL G. FRADKIN
September 1988 to July 1994

LORRAINE WEISS FRANK
July 1997 to present

JOHN HOPE FRANKLIN
July 1976 to February 1979

A. D. FRAZIER, JR.
May 1979 to January 1982

BILLIE DAVIS GAINES
September 1990 to June 1996

EMILY GENAUER
January 1966 to January 1970

A. BARTLETT GIAMATTI
September 1980 to October 1981

ALLAN A. GLATTHORN
February 1968 to January 1974

DARRYL J. GLESS
July 1994 to present

ROBERT F. GOHEEN
March 1966 to January 1968

HANNA HOLBORN GRAY
March 1972 to January 1978

RAMÓN A. GUITIÉRREZ
July 1992 to November 1999

JOSEPH H. HAGAN
July 1992 to November 1999

JAY G. HALL
July 1976 to January 1982

THEODORE HAMEROW
July 1992 to present

CHARLES V. HAMILTON
November 1978 to April 1984

MIKISO HANE
March 1991 to May 1997

GEORGE D. HART
October 1985 to September 1990

JEFFREY HART
February 1972 to September 1977
October 1982 to September 1990

HENRY C. HASKELL
February 1968 to January 1974

EMIL W. HAURY
March 1966 to January 1968

LOUIS J. HECTOR
November 1978 to April 1984

CHARLES P. HENRY
July 1994 to present

WILLIAM A. HEWITT
March 1975 to January 1980

HENRY HIGUERA
September 1990 to July 1997

ADELAIDE C. HILL
March 1966 to January 1968

GERTRUDE HIMMELFARB
July 1982 to September 1988

ROBERT B. HOLLANDER, JR.
June 1974 to January 1980
October 1986 to November 1991

DORIS B. HOLLEB
July 1996 to present

CARL M. HOLMAN
November 1978 to April 1984

THOMAS C. HOLT
July 1994 to April 1997

SIDNEY HOOK
February 1972 to January 1978

PAUL G. HORGAN
March 1966 to July 1970

KAYE HOWE
November 1978 to January 1980

MARTHA C. HOWELL
July 1994 to present

MARIAN B. JAVITS
September 1980 to January 1982

ALICIA JUARRERO
July 1992 to November 1999

DONALD KAGAN
September 1988 to July 1994

NICOLAS KANELLOS
July 1994 to July 2000

LEON R. KASS
July 1984 to March 1991

GEORGE A. KENNEDY
September 1980 to October 1987

LOUISE A. KERR
September 1980 to June 1987

KATHLEEN S. KILPATRICK
July 1984 to August 1989

MARTIN KILSON
February 1972 to January 1978

LESLIE KOLTAI
February 1970 to January 1976

ALAN CHARLES KORS
July 1992 to February 1998

MATHILDE KRIM
February 1969 to January 1974

IRVING KRISTOL
February 1972 to January 1978

JAMES CLAYBURN LAFORCE, JR.
July 1982 to September 1990

ROBERT LAXALT
July 1984 to October 1990

SHERMAN E. LEE
February 1970 to January 1976

JOHN W. LETSON
March 1966 to January 1968

ALBERT W. LEVI
March 1966 to January 1972

EDWARD HIRSCH LEVI
June 1974 to February 1975

BEV LINDSEY
July 1994 to August 1998

HERMAN H. LONG
March 1970 to January 1976

DAVID LOWENTHAL
June 1986 to July 1992

ROBERT M. LUMIANSKY
March 1968 to January 1968

RICHARD W. LYMAN
July 1976 to January 1982

TRUMAN G. MADSEN
June 1974 to January 1980

MICHAEL J. MALBIN
July 1991 to July 1994

HARVEY C. MANSFIELD, JR.
July 1991 to July 1994

DAVID R. MASON
March 1966 to September 1968

GARY L. MCDOWELL
December 1988 to November 1989

SOIA MENTSCHIKOFF
March 1966 to January 1972

William G. Miller
March 1966 to January 1968

Henry A. Moe
September 1966 to January 1970

Jon N. Moline
October 1990 to November 1999

James W. Morgan
February 1968 to January 1974

John C. Murray
March 1966 to August 1967

Jacob Neusner
November 1978 to August 1984

Robert Nisbet
March 1975 to May 1979

Louis W. Norris
February 1970 to August 1970

Mary Beth Norton
November 1978 to July 1984

James C. O'Brien
March 1966 to January 1970

Charles E. Odegaard
May 1966 to January 1972

Paul J. Olscamp
June 1987 to July 1992

Walter J. Ong
February 1968 to January 1974

Anne Paolucci
June 1987 to July 1994

Rosemary Park
March 1970 to January 1976

William R. Parker
February 1968 to October 1968

Ieoh Ming Pei
March 1966 to January 1970

Arthur L. Peterson
March 1970 to January 1976

Eugene B. Power
February 1968 to January 1974

Peggy W. Prenshaw
November 1999 to present

Eugene S. Pulliam
July 1976 to April 1979

Joel Read
November 1978 to April 1984

Emmette S. Redford
January 1966 to January 1970

John S. Reed, Jr.
June 1987 to July 1992

Carolynn Reid-Wallace
February 1988 to January 1992

Francis D. Rhome
September 1980 to June 1987

Rita Ricardo-Campbell
July 1982 to December 1988

Condoleezza Rice
July 1992 to April 1993

Charles Ritcheson
May 1983 to August 1987
June 1988 to September 1990

John Roche
November 1968 to September 1969

Blanchette H. Rockefeller
June 1974 to January 1980

Robert I. Rotberg
July 1994 to present

Joe B. Rushing
July 1976 to January 1982

Ellis Sandoz
July 1982 to December 1988

Philip A. Schaefer
September 1980 to October 1986

James V. Schall
July 1984 to September 1990

John R. Searle
July 1992 to April 1997

Anita Silvers
September 1980 to June 1987

Harold K. Skramstad
July 1994 to present

Jean Vaughan Smith
July 1987 to September 1990

Jeanne J. Smoot
December 1988 to November 1989

Sheldon H. Solow
February 1972 to January 1978

Robert W. Spike
March 1966 to October 1966

Richard R. St. Johns
February 1972 to January 1978

Peter J. Stanlis
July 1982 to June 1988

Leon Stein
November 1978 to July 1984

Robert B. Stevens
October 1986 to July 1992

Theodore W. Striggles
November 1999 to present

Helen M. Taylor
July 1984 to December 1985

Susan E. Trees
May 1997 to present

Frank Vandiver
February 1972 to January 1978

Durward B. Varner
July 1976 to September 1977

Robert E. Ward
February 1968 to January 1974

Dave Warren
May 1979 to January 1982

Alfred E. Wilhelmi
May 1967 to January 1970

Kenny J. Williams
January 1992 to July 1996

Meredith Willson
March 1966 to February 1967

Susan Ford Wiltshire
May 1997 to present

John W. Wolfe
July 1976 to January 1982

Stephen J. Wright
May 1968 to January 1974

William P. Wright, Jr.
June 1988 to July 1994

Harriet M. Zimmerman
December 1978 to April 1984

Credits

8
George Washington, the Father of His Country. Courtesy Library of Congress.

The Hermitage, home of Andrew Jackson, seventh president of the United States. Courtesy Hermitage and Hermitage Ladies Association.

9
George Washington at Verplanck's Point, by John Trumbull, 1782. Courtesy Winterthur Museum.

Monticello, home of Thomas Jefferson, third president of the United States. National Endowment for the Humanities file photo.

Thomas Jefferson (detail) by Charles Willson Peale. Courtesy Independence National Historical Park.

10
Pulling Down the Statue of King George III by William Walcutt, 1854. National Endowment for the Humanities file photo.

11
The Boston Massacre, 1770, by Paul Revere after Henry Pelham. Courtesy American Antiquarian Society.

1787 Fugio cent. National Endowment for the Humanities file photo.

12
Colonel Theodore Roosevelt. Courtesy Theodore Roosevelt Collection, Harvard University.

Dorothy Parker. Courtesy Photofest, New York.

Thomas Jefferson (detail) by Gilbert Stuart. Courtesy National Portrait Gallery, Smithsonian Institution.

Zora Neale Hurston. Courtesy James Agee Film Project.

Booker T. Washington. Courtesy Atlanta History Center.

In shadow: Raising the Chautauqua tent. Courtesy Everett Albers. Photo: Todd Strand.

13
Greek philosopher Plato (left) with the philosopher and scientist Aristotle, from the *School of Athens–Vatican Stanzae* by Raphael. Courtesy Hulton Getty/Archive Photos.

Socrates. Courtesy Hulton Getty/Archive Photos.

14
Young Omahaw, War Eagle, Little Missouri, and Pawnees by Charles Bird King, 1821. Courtesy American Art Museum, Smithsonian Institution.

An *amikuk* mask representing a spirit that lives in the ground, ca. 1900; blue killer whale mask carved by Jim Lake, 1946. Courtesy Anchorage Museum of History.

15
Native dancers. Courtesy Alaska Native Heritage Center.

Last Stand at Little Big Horn, photo by Edward S. Curtis, from *Portraits of North American Indian Life.* Courtesy American Experience.

The Wildshoe family, Nez Perce Indians and prosperous farmers, take a ride in their 1910 Chalmers convertible. Courtesy High Desert Museum.

16
Immigrants arriving at Ellis Island. Courtesy Culver Pictures.

Hester Street, 1898. Courtesy Museum of the City of New York.

17
Shapiro House, exterior and interior. Courtesy Strawberry Banke Museum.

Jamestown church tower as it appeared in excavations in the 1890s. Courtesy Association for the Preservation of Virginia Antiquities.

Children in nineteenth-century Belfast. Courtesy Paul Wagner Productions.

18
Kente cloth. Photo: Don Cole. Courtesy UCLA Fowler Museum of Cultural History.

Carved elephant holding a drum, Ghana. Photo: Don Cole. Courtesy UCLA Fowler Museum of Cultural History.

19
Inside the Slave Ship Albany/Alvarez (detail) attributed to Francis Maynell, seventeenth century. Courtesy National Maritime Museum, Greenwich, England.

20
A Mission Church by Gerrit Greve. © Gerrit Greve/Corbis

Juan Bautista de Anza, artist unknown. Courtesy National Park Service.

21
The church reconstruction at the Mission San Luis de Talimali. Courtesy Florida Archaeology.

Lithograph of the Presidio in San Francisco by V. Adam after Louis Choris, 1820. Courtesy Hulton Getty/Archive Photos.

22
Annie Oakley. Courtesy Denver Public Library, Colorado Historical Society, and Denver Art Museum.

Stephen Ives and Buddy Squires at the Grand Canyon. Courtesy Stephen Ives.

In shadow: *Grassy Bluffs, Upper Missouri* (detail) by George Catlin, 1857–59. Courtesy National Gallery of Art, Washington.

23
Mountain Jack and a Wandering Miner (detail) by E. Hall Martin, 1850. Courtesy Oakland Museum of California.

Gold nuggets. Courtesy Oakland Museum of California.

Elko Ariñak dancers perform at the National Basque Festival. Photo: Charles Blakeslee. Courtesy High Desert Museum.

Lewis and Clark by Frederic Remington. Courtesy Hulton Getty/Archive Photos.

24
The Fall of Richmond on the Night of April 2, 1865 by Currier and Ives. Courtesy Museum of the City of New York and Art Resource.

Civil War recruiting poster. National Endowment for the Humanities file photo.

A Confederate soldier of Ewell's Corps killed May 19, 1864. Courtesy Library of Congress.

25
The Storming of Chapultepec–Quitman's Attack (detail). Courtesy DeGolyer Library, Southern Methodist University.

Jefferson Davis, president of the Confederate States of America. Courtesy Chicago Historical Society.

In shadow: Holograph copy of the Gettysburg Address by Abraham Lincoln. National Endowment for the Humanities file photo.

26
Runaway slave advertisement. Courtesy University of Central Arkansas, Torreyson Library.

Civil War recruitment poster. Courtesy Massachusetts Historical Society.

27
The March on Washington, August 1963. Photo: Declan Hawn. Courtesy National Archives.

Frederick Douglass, ambrotype. Courtesy National Portrait Gallery, Smithsonian Institution.

The Rev. Dr. Martin Luther King, Jr. Photo: Wyatt Lee Walker. Courtesy Texas Commission for the Humanities.

28
Mark Twain, ca. 1870. Courtesy Mark Twain Project at the Bancroft Library, University of California, Berkeley.

29
Walt Whitman, albumen silver print. Courtesy National Portrait Gallery, Smithsonian Institution.

Huckleberry Finn (detail) by Worth Brehm. Courtesy Mark Twain Project at Bancroft Library, University of California, Berkeley.

30
The Woman's Hour Has Struck. Courtesy American Experience.

Eleanor Roosevelt holding the International Declaration of Human Rights, 1949. Courtesy League of Women Voters and American Experience.

31
Equal Rights Amendment march, Washington, D.C., 1971. Courtesy League of Women Voters.

Elizabeth Cady Stanton and Susan B. Anthony. Courtesy Library of Congress.

Margaret Sanger. Courtesy Planned Parenthood–World Population, New York.

Jane Addams. Courtesy University of Illinois at Chicago, University Library, Jane Addams Memorial Collection.

32
Andrew Carnegie. Courtesy Library of Congress and American Experience.

33
Singer Power Machine Sewing Group, 1936–37, photograph by Lewis Hine. Records of the Work Projects Administration. Courtesy National Archives.

Emma Goldman. Courtesy Richard Carter.

Samuel Gompers. Courtesy Samuel Gompers Papers, University of Maryland.

Inside the Jones and Laughlin Steel Corporation, ca. 1880. Courtesy Jones and Laughlin Steel Corporation and Carnegie Library.

Credits

34
World War I recruitment poster. Courtesy Owen Comora Associates.

Wilfred Owen, July 1916. Courtesy Wilfred Owen Trust.

35
Edith Wharton. Courtesy Beinecke Rare Book and Manuscript Library, Yale University.

36
Zelda and F. Scott Fitzgerald. Courtesy Department of Rare Books and Special Collections. Princeton University Library.

Galley page with F. Scott Fitzgerald's corrections, from *Trimalchio*, the first version of *The Great Gatsby*. Courtesy Department of Rare Books and Special Collections, Princeton University Library.

37
Arrow Collar advertisement by J. C. Leyendecker, 1930. Courtesy Granger Collection, New York.

Josephine Baker, ca. 1930. Courtesy Library of America and Smithsonian Institution.

Babe Ruth, photograph by Nikolas Murray, 1927. Courtesy National Portrait Gallery, Smithsonian Institution.

The young Ernest Hemingway. Courtesy John F. Kennedy Library.

38
Migrant Mother, Nopomo, California, 1936, photograph by Dorothea Lange. Courtesy Dorothea Lange Collection, Oakland Museum of California, City of Oakland, Gift of Paul S. Taylor.

39
Dorothea Lange, American photographer, in Texas, photograph by Paul S. Taylor. Courtesy Dorothea Lange Collection, Oakland Museum of California, City of Oakland, Gift of Paul S. Taylor.

President and Mrs. Franklin D. Roosevelt leaving the White House for the Capitol on the occasion of his third inauguration, January 20, 1941. Courtesy Franklin D. Roosevelt Library.

40
General Dwight D. Eisenhower addressing troops before D-Day, June 1944.

Courtesy National Archives. General Douglas MacArthur returns to the Phillippines, 1944. Courtesy National Archives.

41
Image from the poster *Buy War Bonds*. Courtesy Smithsonian Traveling Exhibition Service.

Rosie the Riveter– *We Can Do It*. Courtesy American Experience.

General George C. Marshall. National Endowment for the Humanities file photo.

42
George C. Wallace, governor of Alabama. Photo: Spider Martin Collection. Courtesy American Experience and the Wallace Foundation.

Huey Long addressing the 1932 Democratic convention. Courtesy Public Broadcasting System.

Wallace campaign button, 1968. National Endowment for the Humanities file photo.

43
George C. Wallace, 1940, 1994, 1958. Courtesy American Experience and the Wallace Foundation. 1994 photo: Lloyd Gallman, *Montgomery Advertiser.*

Political map of the United States showing voting patterns for the thirty-sixth Congress, from *Historical Atlas of Political Parties in the United States Congress, 1789–1988.*

44
Thomas A. Edison by Col. Abraham Archibald Anderson. Courtesy National Portrait Gallery, Smithsonian Institution.

Albert Einstein, violinist and physicist. Courtesy Hulton Getty/Archive Photos.

45
Charles Darwin by Charles Henry Jeens. Courtesy Library of Congress.

Lewis Howard Lattimer, ca. 1882. Courtesy Queens Library Foundation, Jamaica, New York.

In shadow: *Incandescent Electric Lighting* by Lewis Latimer. National Endowment for the Humanities file photo.

46
Promotional brochure, U.S. Highway Administration. National Endowment for the Humanities file photo.

Maryland family on U.S. Route 40, Garrett County, Maryland, ca. 1920. Courtesy Maryland Humanities Council and the Maryland State Archives.

47
Advertisement for Aladdin Homes, 1956. Courtesy Clarke Historical Library, Central Michigan University.

Dan Ryan Expressway in Chicago. National Endowment for the Humanities file photo.

48
Ralph Waldo Emerson, albumen silver print by F. Gutekunst, ca. 1875. Courtesy National Portrait Gallery, Smithsonian Institution.

Boaters in Central Park, New York. Courtesy Hulton Getty/Archive Photos.

In shadow: *Lake George* (detail) by John Frederick Kensett. The Metropolitan Museum of Art, Bequest of Maria DeWitt Jesup, 1915. Photograph © 1992 The Metropolitan Museum of Art.

49
The Beeches by Asher B. Durand, 1845. Courtesy The Metropolitan Museum of Art, Bequest of Maria DeWitt Jesup, from the collection of her husband, Morris K. Jesup, 1914. Photograph © 1992 The Metropolitan Museum of Art.

Henry David Thoreau, daguerreotype by Benjamin D. Maxham, 1856. Courtesy National Portrait Gallery, Smithsonian Institution.

Walden Pond in May from Henry David Thoreau's hut. Courtesy Concord Free Public Library.

50
Charlie Parker and Dizzy Gillespie, from *I'll Make Me a World*. Courtesy Blackside, Inc., in association with Thirteen/WNET in New York.

George Gershwin by Edward Steichen, 1929. Courtesy Condé Nast Publications, Inc.

Louis Armstrong, 1959. Courtesy Louis Armstrong House and Archives.

Duke Ellington, 1935. Courtesy Duke Ellington Collection, Smithsonian Institution.

Marian Anderson singing at the Lincoln Memorial, 1939. Courtesy Moorland Spingarn Research Center, Howard University.

51
Still Life with Cello and Bass Fiddle (detail) by Max Beckmann, 1950. Photo: Lee Stalsworth. Courtesy Hirshhorn Museum and Sculpture Garden, Smithsonian Institution, Gift of the Joseph H. Hirshhorn Foundation, 1966.

52
Perimeter Patrol by Michael Crook, 1st Infantry, USA, Vietnam, 1967. Courtesy U.S. Army Center of Military History.

Lyndon B. Johnson takes the oath of office as thirty-sixth president of the United States, November 22, 1963. Courtesy Lyndon B. Johnson Presidential Library.

53
Cover of *Picture Post*: "Our Troops in Korea." Courtesy Hulton Getty/Archive Photos.

Refugees fleeing Communist advances in Vietnam, Cambodia, and Laos. Photo: Gamma-Liaison. Courtesy American Experience.

Protesters against the war in Vietnam, ca. 1970. Photo: Margaret Durrance, Photo Researchers, Inc. Courtesy American Experience.

54
Cape Cod Morning, by Edward Hopper. Courtesy American Art Museum, Smithsonian Institution.

55
Novelist and historian Shelby Foote. Photo: Miriam Berkley.

Eudora Welty. Photo: Curt Richter.

Our Good Earth (detail) by John Steuart Curry, 1940–41. Courtesy College of Agricultural and Life Sciences, University of Wisconsin-Madison.

57
Virginia Festival of the Book 1999 promotional poster, designed by Anya Groner, a student at Western Albemarle High School. Courtesy Virginia Foundation for the Humanities.

58
"La Somme le roi" by Frère Laurent, c.1294. Add. 28162 fol. 10v. Courtesy British Library

59
The Pilgrimage to Canteburry (detail) by Thomas Stothard, 1806–07. Courtesy the Tate Gallery, London, and Art Resource.

Notre Dame de Paris engraving by J. Havill after John Nash. Courtesy Hulton Getty/ Archive Photos.

A knight from William Caxton's *Game of Chess*, ca. 1400. Courtesy Hulton Getty/Archive Photos.

60
Title pages of plays by William Shakespeare, 1597, 1606, 1623. National Endowment for the Humanities file photos.

In shadow: Early seventeenth-century engraving of London. Courtesy Richard Carter.

61
Early seventeenth-century engraving of London showing the Globe Theatre (detail). National Endowment for the Humanities file photo.

Hamlet Apostrophising the Skull, engraving by J. Rogers, after a painting by Sir Thomas Lawrence, R.A., in the National Gallery, London. Courtesy Folger Shakespeare Library.

Queen Elizabeth by an unidentified artist. Courtesy National Maritme Museum, Greenwich, and The Royal Collection, HM Queen Elizabeth II.

62
Sumerian clay tablet. Courtesy Corbis.

A London language school advertisement. Courtesy Hulton Getty/Archive Photos.

63
Japanese building signs in Tokyo. Courtesy Corbis.

Hittite sphinx. Courtesy Corbis.

64
The Creation and the Expulsion of Adam and Eve from Paradise by Giovanni di Paolo ca. 1445. Courtesy The Metropolitan Museum of Art, Robert Lehman Collection, 1975. Photograph © 1981 The Metropolitan Museum of Art.

65
In shadow: Fragments of the Dead Sea Scrolls. National Endowment for the Humanities file photo.

Leaf from a Qu'ran manuscript, in Maghribi script, ca. 1300. Courtesy The Metropolitan Museum of Art, Rogers Fund, 1942. Photograph © 1986 The Metropolitan Museum of Art.

Head of the Buddha, Afghanistan, Gandharan style, fourth–fifth century. Courtesy Victoria and Albert Museum.

66
Death mask of Tutankhamen. National Endowment for the Humanities file photo.

Museum goers at the exhibition, "The Treasures of Tutankhamen," National Gallery of Art, Washington, 1978. National Endowment for the Humanities file photo.

Outer coffin of Henettawy, ca. 1040–991 B.C., Dynasty 21, third intermediate period. Courtesy The Metropolitan Museum of Art, Rogers Fund 1925. Photograph © 1992 The Metropolitan Museum of Art.

In shadow: Winged Isis, Egyptian. Courtesy Museum of Art, Rhode Island School of Design.

67
Relief block: King Mentuhotep II, wearing the White Crown of Upper Egypt. Courtesy The Metropolitan Museum of Art, Gift of the Egypt Exploration Fund, 1907. Photograph © 1994 The Metropolitan Museum of Art.

Winged Isis, Egyptian. Courtesy Museum of Art, Rhode Island School of Design.

Relief found in the Great Hypostyle Hall at Karnak, Egypt. Courtesy University of Memphis.

68
Chao K'uang-yui, first Sung emperor, reigned 960–976. Courtesy East Asian Studies Slide Project, Princeton University.

69
Mao Zedong, former chairman of the Chinese Communist Party. Courtesy America Productions and WGBH Boston.

Playing Weiqi at the Water Pavilion (detail) by Fu Baoshi, 1904–1965. Courtesy The Metropolitan Museum of Art, Gift of Robert Hatfield Ellsworth, in memory of LaFerne Hatfield Ellsworth, 1988. Photograph © 2000 The Metropolitan Museum of Art.

In shadow: *Summer Mountains* (detail) attributed to Ch'u Ting. Courtesy The Metropolitan Museum of Art, Gift of the Dillon Fund, 1973. Photograph © 1988 The Metropolitan Museum of Art.

In shadow: *Poem Written in a Boat on the Wu River*, section 1 (detail). Courtesy The Metropolitan Museum of Art, Gift of John M.Crawford, Jr., in honor of Professor Wen Fong, 1984. Photograph © 1991 The Metropolitan Museum of Art.

70
Head of a woman, perhaps connected to the cult of Demeter and Persephone, late fourth century, B.C. Courtesy Emory University Museum of Art and Archæology.

Roman coins—obverse: bust of Augustus; reverse: heifer. Courtesy Museum of Fine Arts, Boston, and Perseus Project.

In shadow: Interior of the Parthenon. National Endowment for the Humanities file photo.

71
Relief: *Contemplative Athena*, 470–460 B.C. Courtesy Acropolis Museum, Athens.

72
The Hampton Court by Willem van de Velde the Younger. Courtesy Birmingham Museum of Art and Oxford University Press.

73
Indian princes and British army officers in the Hyderabad polo team. Courtesy Hulton Getty/Archive Photos.

Islamic map. Courtesy History of Cartography Project, Department of Geography, University of Wisconsin-Madison.

Double-faced *Enklopion*, Byzantine, late eleventh century–early twelfth century. Courtesy The Metropolitan Museum of Art, Purchase, Lila Acheson Wallace Gift, 1994. Photograph © 1995 The Metropolitan Museum of Art.

Julius Nyerere, prime minister of Tanzania, carried on the shoulders of supporters, after the nation was granted self-government. Courtesy Hulton Getty/Archive Photos.

The Silk Road to China, showing the journey of the Venetian merchant Marco Polo. Courtesy Hulton Getty/Archive Photos.

74
Shadow box collage for My History is America's History. National Endowment for the Humanities file photo.

La Prensa, a Spanish-language newspaper in New York City. National Endowment for the Humanities file photo.

75
Emergency Response and Salvage Wheel. National Endowment for the Humanities file photo.

Crumbling books. Courtesy National Library of Medicine, National Institutes of Health.

76
An illustration to William Blake's poem, *Europe, a Prophecy*, 1794. Courtesy © Leonard de Selva/Corbis.

The Whole Art of Marbling as Applied to Paper, Book Edges, etc., by Charles W. Woolnough, London: G. Bell, 1881. Courtesy The Metropolitan Museum of Art, purchased with income from the Jacob S. Rogers Fund.

Page from the score of Gaspare Spontini's symphony, *I Puntigli delle D.* Courtesy © Archiro Iconografio, S.A./Corbis.

Attendants running toward the Supreme Court, ca. 1954. Courtesy Hulton Getty/Archive Photos.

Colophon

Editor: Mary Lou Beatty

Managing Editor: Meredith Hindley

Art Editor: Richard Carter

Writers: Susan Clark, Rachel Galvin, Susan Q. Graceson, Christine Kalke, Amy Lifson, Ellen Marsh, Larry Myers, Maggie Riechers, Frank Shaw, and Sara E. Wilson.

The book was designed by Crabtree + Company of Falls Church, Virginia. The main text is set in Weiss and the legends are set in Zurich.

For sale by the Superintendent of Documents, U.S. Government Printing Office
Internet: bookstore.gpo.gov Phone: (202) 512-1800 Fax: (202) 512-2250
Mail: Stop SSOP, Washington, DC 20402-0001

ISBN 0-16-050627-1